Thai Cuisine

Mogens Bay Esbensen was born in Denmark in 1930 on a farm where he spent his early years, mostly in the kitchen. He started cooking at the age of four and began classical training when he was fifteen, in Copenhagen.

His career took him to many countries, where he worked in hotels and restaurants. He spent seventeen happy years in Thailand, before coming to Australia in 1976.

During these years he learnt to speak Thai fluently, which meant that many secrets of Thai cuisine, from the simplest home cook's traditional knowledge to the most advanced chef's, were available to him.

Mogens Bay Esbensen became the frontrunner of a group of chefs who shaped the New Cuisine in Australia. He is a master chef, his world-wide experiences are unrivalled and he has a great feeling for transmitting his love of cooking to readers, students and chefs. He believes if you have knowledge, you must share it with others.

Thai Cuisine

MOGENS BAY ESBENSEN

VIKING O'NEIL

Viking O'Neil
Penguin Books Australia Ltd
487 Maroondah Highway, PO Box 257
Ringwood, Victoria 3134, Australia
Penguin Books Ltd
Harmondsworth, Middlesex, England
Viking Penguin, A Division of Penguin Books USA Inc.
375 Hudson Street, New York, New York 10014, USA
Penguin Books Canada Limited
10 Alcorn Avenue, Toronto, Ontario, Canada M4V 1E4
Penguin Books (N.Z.) Ltd
182-190 Wairau Road, Auckland 10, New Zealand

First published by Nelson Publishers 1986
This edition by Penguin Books Australia Ltd 1990

10 9 8 7 6 5 4 3 2

Produced by Viking O'Neil
56 Claremont Street, South Yarra, Victoria 3141, Australia
A Division of Penguin Books Australia Ltd

Typeset by Dovatype
Printed and bound through Bookbuilders Limited, Hong Kong

National Library of Australia
Cataloguing-in-Publication data

Esbensen, Mogens Bay.
Thai cuisine

Includes index.
ISBN 0 670 90311 6.

1. Cookery, Thai. I. Title.

641.59593

CONTENTS

To my mother,
Marcelle Boschan

FOREWORD

The ideas in this book are the personal result of a long love affair with all things Thai. My special love of Thai food comes from the excitement of eating the many and varied dishes served at each meal. In particular, the placement of all the dishes on the table at once, in front of the diner.

The bowl of steaming fragrant rice is the basis of each meal. A steamboat with glowing charcoal embers keeps the soup hot. The stock becomes more concentrated and flavoursome as each person eats from the pot.

The rest of the food is set around in smaller dishes. Guests serve themselves as the meal progresses. The taste of a hot dish is always followed by cooling rice.

Each recipe would serve 6 to 8 people, as each menu has at least five dishes. When only one or two dishes are used, the quantities would need to be doubled. Thai hospitality is renowned, and if unexpected guests arrive one or two extra dishes would be prepared quickly and brought to the table. Thai food is eaten with a spoon and fork, *not* chopsticks. Each person has a plate on which he serves a portion of rice, followed by a taste of each dish. In a family situation, each person dips into the steamboat throughout the meal. Soup bowls are used when there are guests.

Iced water, chilled beer or Thai whiskey is usually served with the meal. In Thailand wine is rarely served with a meal; it's imported and expensive. An ordinary chilled white wine would be most acceptable with spicy food, since the flavour of the food would overpower the delicate bouquet of a great wine. Jasmine tea is served after a meal.

Nam Manao Soda is a popular drink served as a thirst-quencher before and during a meal.

I use Serrano chillis which are usually 2.5 cm (1 inch) long. Be careful with tiny bird's eye chillis, they are much hotter. Add more chillis to your own taste. In Thai food the chilli taste does not last for long on the palate.

INTRODUCTION

My Thai adventure began when I had to choose between a Scandinavian Airlines System posting to Bangkok or Rio de Janeiro. I'd always been fascinated by the Buddhist philosophy and way of life, so I decided to go to Bangkok.

I was to stay for a year, little knowing I would come back to live for seventeen years. The airline would fly to Manila, Tokyo and often Karachi. I would work for one week and have the next free. This left me time to explore Thailand, start to learn the language, to understand the people and their culture. My knowledge of their food grew as I became familiar with the mosaic of their lifestyle.

When I arrived in Bangkok for the first time, in 1959, my first impression was of heat and humidity; it's overpowering until you get used to it. There was an unfamiliar fragrance in the air. Thailand has a smell of its own, pungent and strong. To some newcomers it may be too strong and heavy because it's an aroma they've not experienced before. After a while you get to a point where you've analysed it and grown used to it in the process. Basically it's the smell of garlic and coriander; both are grown prolifically. Along the canals there's the dominant smell of charcoal and burning wood, mingling with sizzling spices.

Gardens around more prosperous houses are filled with flowering trees and shrubs, their perfume enhancing the warm air. Frangipani trees always grow in the temple compounds, their heady flowers have a religious significance and are rarely used in Thai floral decoration.

Flowers play an important part in the daily life of all Thais, and the perfume of flowers is dominated by the sweet scent of jasmine. Women and young girls thread small jasmine buds on to lengths of cotton thread. These garlands are called 'puangmalai' and are placed daily in the spirit house that protects nearly every home in the city.

The spirit house in the garden is neat and clean, decorated daily with fresh flowers, little food offerings, candles and joss sticks. The streets are permeated with this mixture of jasmine, incense, burning charcoal and the frying of garlic and coriander. In the end you adjust to these smells and don't think about them any more, they're just there and part of the atmosphere.

To the Thais, Buddhism is a philosophy which has become a way of life. The simple ritual of the early morning ceremony, offering food to the monks, is repeated by countless families throughout the country. Food of the highest quality is prepared and set on tables outside their houses; steaming pots of freshly cooked rice, curry, prawns and noodles.

The monks pass quietly along the empty streets, wrapped in their vivid saffron robes carrying simple brown bronze-rimmed alms bowls. After the food is served into the bowl, the monk accepts a garland of flowers, jasmine, orchids and lotus blossom. The benefactor then kneels, pressing the palms of his hands against his forehead; a gesture of respect to the monk and to show gratitude for accepting his humble offering.

Thai people believe that by showing generosity towards other men it is possible to 'gain merit' for themselves or deceased relatives, for their future reincarnation, in the hope that they will return in a higher form. Thais don't go to church for prayers and sermons as we do in western religions. Often in a Thai house you'll see a small altar, maybe just a shelf on the wall, where they will have a statue of Buddha. It's a daily ritual to offer a jasmine garland and a bouquet of flowers including lotus blossoms which grow along the canals.

Old Bangkok, with its network of canals, was called 'Venice of the East', now little by little, they have been filled in to make roads, which are hot and dusty. It is the sad price of progress. Houses along the canals are high-set on poles to cope with floods in the monsoon season. There's always a place to shelter when it rains, if you don't mind sharing with numerous roaming dogs and chickens in little cages. Thais believe in animal reincarnation as well.

Bangkok is a city of temples; one for every day of the year. Temples belong to the people and their donations provide the upkeep. Some are neglected, while next door, a splendid new temple is built by a rich man, hoping for the forgiveness of his sins.

Temple fairs to celebrate Buddhist religious days happen continually throughout the year. Special food is cooked, fresh and delicious, and brought to the monks in the morning. At times during the year, when young boys are joining the monastery, there's singing, dancing and special food offerings taking place in the temple compounds.

Temple fairs often become like a circus, with games, stalls and movies in the open air. A highlight will be Likay, folk theatre which originates in the villages. It's a mixture of local politics, satire, fancy costumes, combined with fun and laughter, similar to Chinese opera. Sometimes there's a shadow puppet show for the children who are watched over by their elder brothers and sisters.

At a temple fair there will be dozens of food stalls supplied from mobile kitchens; consisting basically of a charcoal burning brick stove holding the steaming cooking pots. The versatile stove is quickly turned into a barbecue with a wire rack and the smell of spicy satay, chicken and pork, fills the air. There's an endless variety of food; golden spit roasted chicken, heavy black pots filled with simmering curries; beef in a rich sauce or wild boar on festive occasions.

Other stalls provide fresh fruit which is the usual end to a Thai meal, and it's grown all year round. Sweets are eaten as a snack, between meals. Thais eat all the time and they love snacks!

Most of their sweets are based on coconut milk or cream and agar agar, the gelatine of the tropics. Agar agar has a slightly crunchy texture and is cooling to the palate. Thais like to drink 'oleung', a style of iced coffee taken with a snack. The drink is a mixture of roasted corn, spices and some coffee. Boiling water is poured over this mixture in a muslin bag and it's dunked until black enough. They add condensed or evaporated milk and it's always served sweet.

It's traditionally Thai, a lovely, cooling, soothing drink, not pungent like strong roasted pure coffee. On railway stations boys run along the platform, and sell it in little plastic bags with a straw. With 'oleung' and a few sweets you'll last happily until the next station.

Cold fruit drinks and juices come in psychedelic colours and are poured over finely shaved ice, like snow, never over ice-blocks. Sugar-cane juice is popular and delicious. The cane is fed through an old-style washing mangle; it's a simple sugar which is nourishing, easily digested and absorbed readily into the bloodstream for instant energy. Fragrant pineapples are pressed in the same way.

Tangerine trees grow all around Bangkok and give a perfumed juice, with more flavour than oranges. Tamarind is an important flavour in many Thai dishes. The trees grow around temples and when the fruit is ripe the juice is squeezed and used constantly in cooking. The flavour is slightly sour and vinegar is not a successful substitute. Lime juice is also an essential Thai ingredient and lemons are practically unknown.

Part of the magic of Bangkok is the many and varied markets. In the early 1960s there were three main markets and I always went to the one by the river, near the old Oriental Hotel, called Bang Rak. It was the market chosen by foreigners and their maids, who would shop for a better choice of ingredients

In Chinatown, markets specialise in vegetables, brought by boat from the country, fresh fish and Chinese ingredients. The stalls are crammed into narrow alleys, jammed close to each other, covered by awnings to protect their goods from sudden tropical showers.

In the fish market there's an overpowering smell of dried fish which is separate from the fresh varieties. It combines with spices, little red onions like shallots, and fresh green peppercorns on stalks. Tiny freshwater fish are cleaned, dried on a bamboo mat in the sun and served for breakfast. There's not much meat but they're rich in protein. One or two are crisped over a charcoal fire and served with a bowl of watery boiled rice, topped with finely chopped chilli and a dash of fish sauce.

Thais eat a lot of fish, mainly caught in the Gulf of Thailand, but also found in ponds and canals. Prawns, squid and crabs with their claws tied together are piled on ice in wicker baskets; eels and catfish squirm in buckets. Fishwives shout at the top of their voices to attract the customers' attention, their wrinkled faces stained with betel nut. Wriggling fish are taken home in plastic bags to be cooked later in the day. Catfish is grilled over an open fire to give it a distinctive smoky flavour.

Thais are careful when buying meat as they don't trust refrigerators. Most people don't have one; if they do it's filled with soft drink. They would rather go back to the market for a second time to buy fresh meat; once it's been chilled they would not know how old it is. Thais like meat that is warm to touch and then they're sure it's fresh. There is pork and beef, and a lot of water buffalo; it's fresh and warm, but not particularly tender. Meat is tenderised in the cooking process.

Outside the market there are food stalls to catch the passing trade, and again the food is cooked on a charcoal burner. Street stalls offer the inveterate Thai snacker a multitude of taste sensations. A typical snack is a type of crêpe, made from a coconut and rice flour mixture, cooked on a cast-iron plate until thin and crisp. Filled with shredded coconut, pumpkin, chopped onion, peanuts and bean paste, it is folded in half, served and eaten at once.

Other stalls offer steamed delicacies, cooked on muslin over boiling water, filled with a paste of chopped chilli, salt and sugar. The texture is crunchy and hot; it has to be *hot*. With the enormous variety of fruit, stalls display the best in season. Succulent pineapple on sticks, to munch as you walk along; pomelo, star apple, jackfruit, sapodillo, custard apple. Exotic tropical fruit like mangosteen with its creamy segments encased in a hard purple shell, rambutan covered with soft, red spikes and tasting like a lychee; the evil smelling durian, whose taste becomes addictive. This is not part of a meal. Thais enjoy the variety and social side of a street snack.

Street vendors set up their gaily coloured canvas-topped trolleys for the lunch-time crowd. Office workers leave their buildings, and head for their favourite vendor, who has a few tables and chairs near his portable stove. He always has a pot of stock simmering and an open fire for the wok. His trolley holds a cabinet with shelves displaying all types of noodles; egg noodles, glass noodles and the flat, wide variety, all freshly made. Roasted duck and chicken, redolent with spices, hang appetisingly at eye level, bowls filled with slices of pork, peeled prawns, cleaned mussels, fish pieces and piles of fresh, chopped vegetables.

We would call this *mis en place* in a western kitchen. All ingredients are prepared at home and brought to the site by the vendor. The customer makes his choice and it is prepared quickly in front of him. Noodles are dipped in and out of the boiling stock, placed into a bowl, topped with sliced chicken or pork, a few prawns, a little stock and garnished with chilli peanut sauce and coriander leaves. Lunch is fresh, instant, delicious and eaten on the spot.

Another traditional Thai lunch is 'Kao pat', fried rice cooked in a wok, with your choice of ingredients; roast chicken or duck, shredded pork, marinated fish or pink glistening prawns. If you have to rush back to the office, your lunch is wrapped in a banana leaf, Nature's most adaptable wrapper. In the markets banana leaves are sold in big bunches by the kilo, and cut into required sizes. Everyone grows banana trees around their houses in Bangkok, from plantains, sugar bananas to the tiny egg bananas; they're used in all types of cooking.

Thais look forward to their evening meal, freshly cooked and served. This is what makes Thai food so exciting; the flavours are fresh and unspoiled. An everyday evening meal, called Gub Kao consists of cooked rice, a soup dish (Gaeng), a spicy salad (Yum), lots of fresh cooked vegetables sprinkled with lime juice and served with dipping sauces, stir-fried pork or chicken curry. Dinner is finished with fruit or sticky rice with coconut milk.

Fresh herbs are used constantly in cooking and grown everywhere. Each house or dwelling, no matter how cramped or crowded, even with no land of its own, has herbs. Little tins growing tree basil and lemon grass are tied to the sides of houses or on the windowsill.

Makrut, a little bush that looks a bit like a lime, produces a fragrant leaf that is used in soups, curries and fish puddings. The plant always looks sad and sorry because the Thais keep picking the leaves. It has fruit that looks like wild lime; all skin with no juice; its skin is finely peeled and used to flavour food. Even though makrut is sold in the market, Thais like to have it growing at home. Herbs scent the air around the house and you'll always see pots of simple orchids to brighten their surroundings.

When I first came to Bangkok I lived in a little wooden bungalow right out of a Somerset Maugham novel, with two bedrooms and a bathroom upstairs and a living- and diningroom with a bar downstairs. I had a little garden with mango trees, some orchids and a spirit house. The greatest luxury was to have a maid to cook and wash, and a gardener.

After the Bangkok posting I went back to Denmark, but not for long. Thailand again beckoned me, with a job as food and beverage manager at the Rama Hotel. Soon I was involved in setting up an international resort at Pattaya, then a sleepy fishing village, with a few bungalows and shops, but no accommodation.

The next exciting step in my career happened in 1965 when I opened a restaurant called the *Two Vikings*, together with my friend, Preben Vinther. It took us six weeks to design and convert a huge old Chinese house into the restaurant. It was the golden age of Bangkok, when every major international company was represented and most foreigners lived and entertained in western style.

I returned to my profession as a chef and recalled my experiences with Mr Eiler Jorgensen, Copenhagen's best known chef and restaurateur. He was the Ferdinand Point of Denmark. I learned from him about style and certainly more about cooking. I wanted to create a similar ambience in the *Two Vikings*; it had to be like stepping into another world.

Cars swept along the driveway through the tropical garden, up to an awning sheltering the entrance. Marble steps led to the foyer, a central room, decorated with a tableau of perfumed flowers and exotic fruit. Each room leading from the foyer was designed in a different Scandinavian theme and decorated individually.

'The Inn' had shutters painted with Danish folklore, old wooden tables and benches. I collected antique Siamese maps and hung them on the walls of the 'Mermaid Room', together with paintings related to a maritime theme. Eight guests dined in the 'Safari Room' at an iron table with an inlaid mosaic top; from the ceiling hung saffron muslin, held in place by tent poles. The garden was the focus of the 'Hamlet Room' and the 'Oval Room' walls were decorated with a collection of porcelain botanical plates.

A staircase led to a private diningroom, seating 22, with an adjoining lounge for cocktails and after-dinner coffee. The men would always stay at the table for port and cigars. Around the walls I hung my hand-embroidered herbal and botanical tapestries, 24 in all. In those days I painted and sculpted, and always found a corner in one of the rooms for my work. The kitchen and menu was my domain while Preben was at the 'front of house'.

I sold out to my partner in 1972 and for a change of scene started a small orchid farm on land I cleared along the coast from Pattaya. After two years I went back to the food business as a consultant to the Bangkok Hyatt Hotel and whilst on a promotional trip to the Hyatt Kingsgate I discovered Sydney.

It was time for change; I wanted to cook and be creative, not work in an office talking on the phone and answering letters. *Pavilion on the Park* became my new obsession with the opportunity to design the interior of a new restaurant, plan the menu and establish the kitchen. The project succeeded and *Pavilion on the Park* became the prettiest and perhaps the most popular restaurant in Sydney.

The late 1970s was a time for revolution in cooking, and certainly in the understanding of dining-out in Australia. As a result of living so many years in Asia I developed my own style of honest cooking; I call it 'ma cuisine'. The food I prepare and serve is much lighter and has more visual appeal than most traditional western food. Those years gave me a natural understanding of simple light cooking and artistic presentation.

I used to lunch regularly on the terrace at *Butler's* in Potts Point and was overwhelmed by its spectacular view across the city skyline. The restaurant is part of two tiny old houses, built in 1850. When I bought *Butler's* in 1979, I planned an international menu, having lived in different countries and soaked up their atmospheres.

Butler's became my life and still is although I succumbed again to the hedonistic lifestyle of the tropics. On a holiday in Port Douglas, in far north Queensland, I discovered the *Nautilus*, with its charming terrace shaded by tall palms; the warm air perfumed with frangipani and jasmine. I was at home.

My life has taken a full circle; I'm living in a cottage, set in a lush green garden, under the shining sun. I am doing the things I love best of all; cooking and living in the tropics.

Most of the herbs and exotic fruits used in this book are growing in my garden at the *Nautilus*. I believe that those of us who love to cook and experiment with new dishes should keep asking for rare and exotic ingredients. This will eventually create a supply.

Items like green pawpaw and green mangoes are found in oriental stores, along with fresh lemon grass, kalangal (lesser ginger), fresh peppercorns and a variety of chillis.

In my profession, I feel that if you have knowledge it is essential to share it with others. There can be no secrets. Most techniques have been tried somewhere along the line.

This book is the result of requests from many people; students in my cooking classes, guests at my restaurant, friends and colleagues. It has been made possible through the enormous help and encouragement of

Delphine Zwar. Michael Cook's photographic expertise has brought the colour and warmth of the dishes to life. He took all the photographs in natural light at the *Nautilus*. My thanks go to Kit Robinson for his assistance in preparing intricate dishes and the carved fruit found in the photographs.

The menus are compiled from my favourite dishes which I often serve to friends and guests. It is my interpretation of the Thai style of cooking; some dishes are classic Thai, the rest are my own, adapting the exotic requirements of Thai cooking to suit the western palate.

This is a book for friends who love cooking and cannot stop; always searching for excitement in taste and texture, exotic ingredients and new dishes. I am sharing my love with you, always remembering that successful cooking is the result of using quality ingredients.

Mogens Bay Esbensen

GLOSSARY

BASIL

There are three types of basil used in Thai cooking:

BAI HORAPA — nearest to sweet European basil and used in Thai curries.
BAI MANGLAK — has tiny leaves, similar to Greek basil. It is sprinkled over salads and used in soups.
BAI GRAPAO — leaves are narrow and reddish-purple in colour. It is used cooked in meat and fish dishes, leaving a hot taste on the palate.

European basil can be used as a substitute in any dish. However, it is fun to grow different varieties and experience their taste.

CARDAMOM
LOOK KRA-VAN

Cardamom comes from a herbaceous perennial, native to India. The off-white fruit capsule contains black seed, both of which are used to flavour and garnish Thai dishes.

CHILLI PEPPERS
PRIK

Chillis are members of the capsicum family and were introduced to Thai cuisine by the Portuguese in the 16th century. The Thai word for chilli is Prik Thes, meaning foreign pepper. The original pepper, Prik Thai, was used before the arrival of the little hot 'foreigners', which have now become synonymous with Thai cooking. The large chilli, Prik Chee Fa, is used for dried chilli powder, in cayenne pepper and for medicinal products. Chillis have been known and used for centuries to treat high blood pressure and cholesterol. Prik E Noo Kaset, is a new chilli imported from Mexico with longer pods than the native Prik E Noo Suan, the bird's eye type which is hot. They are also known as Serrano chillis. Prik Leung or Yellow Chillis, are often called Scotch Bonnets, because of their shape, and are very hot. Prik Yuak, or Capsicum Annum Grossum are generally known as capsicum, sweet peppers or bell peppers. As newcomers to Thai cuisine, they are often used for stuffing, stir-fried and in salads.

CINNAMON
OB CHUEY

I have a handsome cinnamon tree growing in my garden. Although cinnamon bark is commonly used for flavouring, I use fresh leaves from the

Clockwise from top: Limes; garlic; shallots; on plate: Makrut leaves, tiny eggplants for curry; cherry tomatoes; eggplants. Szechuan peppers; dried red chillis; cardamom; turmeric (ground); turmeric root; dried Galanga Laos, cinnamon leaf; cinnamon bark; fresh Galanga Laos; bitter gourd; eggplants (purple and white); lemon grass; basil.

tree for a definite spicy taste. Cinnamon bark often discolours food, so I use the leaves for a more gentle flavour, especially in ice-cream.

CLOVES
KRAN PLOO

Cloves are the dried flowerbuds of an evergreen tree, native to the Molucca Islands. Fresh clove flowers are a luxury to chew and you do not need a toothache to enjoy them.

COCONUT
MAPRAO

The most important palm grown in the lowland tropical areas is the coconut. Every part of it is utilised. The fronds are used for thatching houses and for weaving mats and baskets, the sticks for satay.

The coconut itself has a fibre covering, used for making ropes, door mats and brushes. The inside meat is dried for copra, from which an oil is removed to make soap, cosmetics and candles. Young green coconuts contain refreshing juice, a thirst-quenching hot weather drink; the hard shells are made into utensils, cups and ladles.

The meat of the mature coconut is grated for coconut milk. Pour 500 mls (2 cups) of boiling water over 1 kilogram of grated coconut and allow to stand until cool. Squeeze the grated coconut well with your hands to remove the milk and strain through muslin. This should give you 4–5 cups of coconut milk; about 1 litre. When it is cold, cream will have formed on the surface. Should a recipe call for coconut cream, skim the required amount from the top and use the remainder as coconut milk. Make up the same amount by using unsweetened desiccated coconut when you don't have fresh coconuts. Experiment with brands of tinned coconut milk to find the best variety. Make sure there are no preservatives or thickening agents added.

CORIANDER
PAK CHEE

Coriander is also known as Cilantro and Chinese parsley. It is an easily-grown herb and most important to Thai cooking. Buy bunches of the whole plant as the root and stem are necessary ingredients. The bright green fragrant leaves are used as a garnish. Dried seeds are not used unless specified. Marco Polo brought coriander to south-east Asia from the Mediterranean via China.

Utensils for Thai cooking.

CUMIN
YEE RAA

Cumin is an annual, native to Egypt, with small ridged light-brown seeds. They are similar to fennel and caraway, but taste quite different. The seeds must be toasted to release the flavour, and are used in Thai cooking to make curry paste.

RED CURRY PASTE

1 cup shallots (red onions), chopped
1 cup garlic, chopped
1 cup lemon grass, tender parts only, chopped
2 tablespoons coriander root, chopped
2 tablespoons fresh galangal, laos root, fresh or dried, chopped
2 teaspoons peppercorns
2 teaspoons coriander seeds, roasted
2 teaspoons cumin seeds, roasted
2 teaspoons lime zest or makrut, grated
1 teaspoon nutmeg, ground
1 teaspoon mace
20 to 30 dried red chillis
4 tablespoons shrimp paste (kapee)
2 tablespoons salt

Grind dry spice ingredients in a spice mill. Add powder and remaining ingredients to a food processor bowl and mix to a smooth paste.

This is a large quantity but keeps well in a sealed jar in the refrigerator. The more dried chillis which are added, the redder the colour. If you remove the seeds from the chillis, you can increase the number of chillis without making the paste hotter.

GREEN CURRY PASTE

Use the same ingredients as for Red Curry Paste substituting fresh green chillis instead of dried red chillis. Again, by removing the seeds from the fresh green chillis you can increase the amount. Add chilli leaves, coriander leaves or spinach to increase the green colour.

EGGPLANT
MA-KHUA

Eggplants of many shapes and sizes are grown in Thailand. The tiny, berry-sized eggplant, Ma-Khua Puang, is used in Nam-Prik, the chilli sauce and to garnish green curries. The long eggplant, Ma-Khua Yao, is mostly green, but sometimes purple or white. It is cooked or grilled as in Yam Ma-Khua. The small round eggplant, green, yellow and white, is eaten raw with Nam Prik. They have an interesting texture but little taste. The larger western aubergine can be used in Thai cooking, but lacks the texture of the smaller variety.

FISH SAUCE
NAM PLA

Fish sauce is an essential ingredient to Thai cuisine. It is a thin, translucent brown sauce the colour of sherry, made from fish, shrimps and crabs. The fish is salted and fermented in jars, and during the slow process, the liquid is extracted, bottled and left to cure. Fish sauce was known in early Roman days and was highly prized at Caesar's court. The Romans used Muria, a salty fish liquid substance drawn from fermented tunny fish. Another fish sauce was imported by the Romans from the Phoenicians, who in turn brought it from the Sudrans when they came back from the Far East. Fish sauce is rich in vitamin B and protein. The natural protein additive, used by Nature in the formation of fishbone, may prolong life, retarding the aging process. Fish sauce has a delicious flavour and can be used as a salt substitute in western cooking.

GALANGAL/LAOS
KA

Galangal is also known as lesser ginger or Siamese ginger and is a relative of the ginger family. The rhizome is pale yellow with pink knobs and sprouts; the flavour is a cross between ginger and cardamom. Also known as Laos, it can be found in Asian food shops, dried or powdered.

HOT SOY SAUCE

1 litre (4 cups) soy sauce, light
10 chillis, long

Roast the chillis over fire or under broiler until they are black all over. Add to soy sauce, bottle, and allow to stand for at least a week. Use to flavour salads.

KAFFIR LIME
MAKRUT

By far the most fragrant leaf used in Thai cooking, Makrut is a member of the citrus family. The leaf has the combined aromatics of lemon verbena, geranium and lemon. Finely chop the leaves to add pungent flavour to soup, fish pudding and curry. The fruit resembles a knobbly lime; the rind is grated and used to flavour many dishes. This can be found in a dried form in Thai food shops, and is called Pew Makrut.

LEMON GRASS
TAKRAI

Lemon grass is probably the best-known herb used in Thai cooking and gives a characteristic 'lemony' taste to many dishes. The plant looks like long grey-green grass and is related to citronella. It can be found in health food shops, dried, cut into pieces or powdered. It adds flavour to curry pastes, soups and salads and is at its best when fresh; an indispensable ingredient. Lemon peel can be used as a substitute.

MACE
DAWK CHAND

Mace is the orange outer covering of nutmeg, the fruit of an evergreen tree and is used to flavour curry paste.

MARINATED STEM GINGER
KING DONG

1 kg (2 lbs) young fresh green ginger
500 g (1 lb) sugar
500 mls (2 cups) white vinegar
1 lt (4 cups) water

Peel skin from ginger. If it is not so young, soak overnight in water. Slice ginger as thin as possible. Combine sugar, vinegar and water, bring to boil, add ginger and simmer for 40 minutes. Remove from heat and allow to cool.

Fill sterilised jars and store in a cool place. Leave for at least a week before using. Try to make marinated ginger when the fresh young shoots are available.

For a lovely pink tinge to the ginger add 1–2 dried red chillis to the vinegar syrup.

Marinated ginger is excellent combined in salads, sauces and served with ice-cream.

NUTMEG
LOOK CHAND

Nutmeg is a fragrant nut used to make curry paste.

PANDANUS/SCREW PINE
BAI TOEY HOM

A tropical herbaceous plant, also known as screw pine, pandanus leaf is used for flavouring and colour. It has a sweet, nutty flavour when added to rice and sweets, and wrapped around meat. The dried leaf is sold in Asian food shops, and there is no substitute.

PASTE FOR FISH PUDDING
KREUNG-HO MOK

6 green chillis, chopped
6 shallots (red onions), chopped
6 cloves garlic, chopped
2 stalks lemon grass, tender part only, chopped
1 teaspoon fresh green peppercorns
1 teaspoon tumeric powder
1 teaspoon shrimp paste (kapee)
1 tablespoon galangal root, dried, chopped

Combine all ingredients in a food processor and blend until a fine smooth paste has formed. Ideally, the paste should be pounded with mortar and pestle. Store in a sealed jar and refrigerate.

PEPPER — PIPER NIGRUM
PRIK THAI

In the 18th century, Cambodia paid taxes to the King of Thailand. The payment was made in cardamom and beeswax. In return the King of Cambodia received pepper and cloth. At that time Cambodia was known in Europe as 'La Region des Montagnes de Cardamom' — the region of the spice mountains.

Pepper was discovered growing wild on the Malabar coast of India. It was cultivated in Java and found by Marco Polo in the 13th century. Moslems brought it to Sumatra and in the 16th century trading ships carried pepper to the Malay Peninsula.

During the age of discovery, pepper became worth its weight in gold. Columbus thought he had reached his goal when he found vines of small dark berries growing in the West Indies. It was allspice.

In April 1797, a schooner named *Rajah* sailed into New York harbour. Its cargo was 75 tons of black pepper, the profit on which was 700 per cent. The captain refused to let anyone know where he found the pepper. Gradually, his route was established and trading in pepper began.

Piper Nigrum is a vine which grows on trees or on wooden poles. It can be grown easily in the tropics and as a secondary crop in plantations. When peppercorns are freshly picked and green, they are far superior in flavour to the dried black variety. White peppercorns are picked when ripe, their skins removed and the kernels dried. Fresh green peppercorns are easily crushed to release their flavour; spread on steak, fish, added to a sauce or salad, they are a culinary delight.

PICKLED GARLIC
KRATIEM DONG

Garlic, pickled in vinegar, can be found in most Asian food stores. It is made
from young green garlic, left in whole bulbs as the skins are soft and easy to
eat. Whenever I see young garlic in the markets I buy all there is because it
is hard to find. Green garlic tops make the most delicious soup and whole
bulbs can be roasted with baby chicken and spring lamb.

1 litre (4 cups) water
250 mls (1 cup) vinegar
5 tablespoons sugar
1 tablespoon salt

Mix all ingredients together and bring to boil. Separate garlic bulbs into
cloves, peeling skin if it is hard. Leave skin on cloves if garlic is young. Add
garlic to boiling vinegar mixture and bring back to boil for 1 minute.

Pour into jars and store in a cool place for at least a week. The flavour
improves with time.

PRESERVED SALTED EGGS
KAI KEM

Salted eggs are used from time to time in Thai dishes, as many people do
not have refrigeration. Hard-boiled salted eggs are served with snacks and
the yolk is used for a dry curry, Prik King, a favourite amongst the Thais.

2 dozen large eggs
2 litres (8 cups) water
3 tablespoons salt

To make brine, bring water and salt to boil for 5 minutes. Allow to cool.
Carefully place eggs in an earthenware crock or glass jar with lid. Pour cold
brine to cover eggs and store for at least 4 weeks. Use as required.

RICE
KAO

Rice is the basis of all Thai meals, served white and fluffy. The Thais use two
varieties of the grain; long and short. Short grain or glutinous rice is often
cooked with coconut milk and called sticky rice. The short grain is a staple
part of the diet in northern Thailand, in Laos and Cambodia, and even
Burma. It is eaten by rolling a small ball in your fingers and then dipping it
into a spicy sauce. Long grain comes in many varieties, and the best Thai
cooks always choose Mali rice, which has the scent of jasmine.

STEAMED FRAGRANT RICE
KAO HORM MALI
To cook Thai long grain rice:

4 cups long grain rice

1.25 l water (5 cups).

After rinsing rice under cold running water until clear, add to water in a heavy based saucepan. Bring to boil, stir well and reduce heat to simmer. Cover with a lid and cook for 12 minutes over low heat.

Remove from heat and stand for 10 minutes, still covered. Fluff up rice with a fork or chopsticks. This recipe is Steamed Fragrant Rice, to be found in most menus.

SHRIMP PASTE
KAPEE
This pungent paste may smell unpleasant but it is essential to many Thai dishes. It is a rich source of protein and vitamin B; made by pounding fermented salted shrimps. It should be stored in a tightly sealed jar, and when cooked there is no trace of the odour.

STAR ANISE
POY KAK BUA
Pungent star anise is sold in Asian and health food shops as dried flowerets or powdered. It is used to flavour bland rice and pork dishes, and is an essential spice in Chinese cooking.

TAMARIND
MAK KAM
Tamarind is a majestic tree with fine fern-like leaves. Also called a Sudran date, the tree grows to an old age. Its timber is hard and used to make chopping blocks. The fruit is like a big bean pod and is dark brown when ripe. Thai people will eat the fruit when green, but it is the brown pulp that is used for cooking. Tamarind pulp can be found in Asian food stores already prepared.

To make tamarind water I use 200 g (8 oz) of pulp combined with 500 mls (2 cups) hot water. Squeeze together to remove the juice, allow to stand for 1 hour and strain off juice. Tamarind concentrate should be used with caution, dissolving one part to three parts of water.

Tamarind gives a slightly sour flavour to Thai curries, fish and meat dishes.

WATER CHESTNUTS
HAEW
Water chestnuts are a corm, grown in a hedge around swampy areas in Thailand and are most plentiful in the monsoon season. Whole or sliced water chestnuts are available in tins and may be found in Asian food shops. They have a refreshing, crunchy texture for which there is no substitute.

EQUIPMENT FOR THAI COOKING

Most interested cooks have a well equipped kitchen in which to do Thai cooking, however, some additions are essential.

Bamboo steamer

Wok — perfect for frying, stir-frying, and with added water it makes a base for your steam basket.

Mortar and pestle — used for classic cuisine, although almost replaced by the food processor and spice mill.

Chopping board — keep an extra one for chillis.

Coconut grater — useful if you can get fresh coconuts.

Chinese cleaver or large kitchen knife.

Jelly moulds — for agar agar desserts.

Cast-iron pan for making coconut pancakes — Kanom Kluk. (ÆBLESKIVE PANDE BY COPCO) .

VOCABULARY

Basil	Bai Horapa
Cardamom	Look Kra-Van
Chilli	Prik
Cinnamon	Ob Chuey
Cloves	Kran Ploo
Coconut	Maprao
Coriander	Pak Chee
Cumin	Yee Raa
Curry paste	Krueng Gaeng Ped
Eggplant	Ma-Khua
Fish sauce	Nam Pla
Galangal or Laos	Ka
Kaffir lime	Makrut
Lemon grass	Takrai
Mace	Dawk Chand
Nutmeg	Look Chand
Pandanus or Screw Pine	Bai Toey Hom
Pepper	Prik Thai
Rice	Kao
Shrimp paste	Kapee
Star anise	Poy Kak Bua
Tamarind	Mak Kam
Water chestnut	Haew

LUNCH WITH MICHEL ROUX

What do you serve a world-renowned chef when you invite him to lunch? This was my problem when Michel Roux — who with his brother Albert, runs two 3-star restaurants: *The Waterside Inn* at Bray on the Thames and *Le Gavroche* in London — accepted my invitation.

When Michel visited Australia, he came to *Butler's* to cook a special dinner and launch his new cookbook. Traditionally my Sunday lunches have always been Thai food, so I decided that lunch with Michel would be no exception. I chose the following menu, and to my delight found that he enjoyed Thai cuisine as much as I do. He made a point of stopping in Bangkok to eat Thai food at the Oriental Hotel. My guest of honour understood more than most the intricate flavours and delicate use of herbs.

The warm clear waters of the Gulf of Thailand teem with seafood and fish. In Australia we have just as much choice so I served a salad of lobster with mint and lemon grass, as a refreshing start to our lunch. Moreton Bay or Balmain bugs are just as good; we called them slipper lobster in Thailand. The delicate meat needs just a quick dip into boiling water, creating a firmer texture. The marinade does the rest of the 'cooking'. A salad of salmon roe on buttercrunch lettuce leaves preceded the warm dishes.

Fried Thai fish cakes, crunchy and golden brown, are a traditional treat, especially good for parties. Served with the cool and crunchy, spicy cucumber salad there is a mingling of taste sensations. My true favourite is steamed fish pudding, wrapped in the versatile banana leaf; its smooth, creamy consistency spiked with lime or basil leaves and steamed to perfection. Soft lettuce leaves make a perfect substitute for those who don't have bananas growing in their garden.

The chicken is cooked in green curry paste (see glossary); a blend of spices coloured with herbs and green chillis is served with steaming bowls of rice. In Thailand this curry would include tiny green eggplants, which retain their colour when cooked and are added for texture. Pickled in brine, these eggplants are sold in a glass jar in Asian food shops. Add half a cup to this recipe, remembering to rinse well in cold water to remove the brine. Chickpeas make a good alternative, soaked in water overnight and cooked with the curry. Don't use green peas, they have no taste or texture. As a soothing finale to a perfect blending of Thailand's most subtle dishes I served the traditional mangoes with sticky rice.

YAM GOONG
SALAD OF LOBSTER WITH MINT AND LEMON GRASS

YAM KAI PLA DOOK
FISH ROE SALAD

TORD MAN PLA
FRIED THAI FISH CAKES

YAM THAENG KWA
SPICY CUCUMBER SALAD

GAENG KEO WAN GAI
CHICKEN CURRY

HO MOK PLA
STEAMED FISH PUDDING

KAO HORM MALI
STEAMED FRAGRANT RICE

KAO NIEO MAMUANG
MANGOES WITH STICKY RICE

YAM GOONG
SALAD OF LOBSTER WITH MINT AND LEMON GRASS

500 g (1 lb) raw lobster tails, Moreton Bay bugs, slipper lobster
1 stalk lemon grass
6 limes or 2 lemons, juice only
2–3 fresh red chillis
1 cup mint leaves
20 ml (1 tablespoon) fish sauce
mint sprigs to garnish

Cut lemon grass into thin slices. Squeeze the juice of limes or lemons and mix with lemon grass. Chop red chillis and add to juice, together with mint leaves and fish sauce.

   Shell lobster tails and slice across body. Place in strainer and dip quickly into boiling water. While still warm add lobster to sauce and leave to marinate for 30 minutes.

   Garnish with mint sprigs.

YAM KAI PLA DOOK
FISH ROE SALAD

The fresh roe from catfish (pla dook) and that of the carp is delicious. Use salmon roe for this salad. When a fresh catfish is used, it is grilled before removing the roe. The flesh from the fish is then removed from the bones and fried until crisp.

220 g (7 oz) pink salmon roe
220 g (7 oz) flesh from firm fish, cut into thin strips
oil for frying
5 shallots (red onions) sliced thinly
juice of 3 limes
2.5 cm (1 inch) fresh green ginger, finely sliced
25 ml (1 tablespoon) fish sauce
leaves of buttercrunch lettuce
thinly sliced red chillis and coriander leaves for garnish

Heat oil and fry strips of fish until crisp. Remove and drain on paper towel. Fry shallots until crisp and drain on paper towel. Combine salmon roe with lime juice to loosen the grains, adding fish sauce and ginger. Toss together with crisp fish and shallots. Serve on lettuce leaves, garnished with chillis and coriander leaves.

TORD MAN PLA
FRIED THAI FISH CAKES

500 g (1 lb) fish fillets
1 red capsicum, chopped
2 red chillis, chopped
2 cloves garlic, chopped
1 stalk lemon grass, tender part only, chopped
20 ml (1 tablespoon) fish sauce
125 ml (½ cup) coconut milk
1 whole egg
125g (4 oz) snake beans or string beans
peanut or vegetable oil for frying

Cut fish into small pieces. Place capsicum, chillis, garlic, lemon grass and fish sauce into food processor bowl and blend to a paste. Add fish pieces to paste and blend well. Mix to a smooth paste with added coconut milk and egg. Place mixture in a bowl. Slice beans finely into 3mm (⅛ inch) slices and stir into fish paste. Chill in refrigerator overnight or for at least 2 hours.

Heat oil in frying pan. Shape chilled paste into small patties with the help of a spoon. Fry in oil until crisp and brown, turning once. Drain on paper towels.

Serve with spicy cucumber salad.

YAM THAENG KWA
SPICY CUCUMBER SALAD

2 medium cucumbers
30 g (1 tablespoon) sugar
40 ml (2 tablespoons) white vinegar
2 red chillis, finely minced
50 g (2 oz) crushed roasted peanuts
2 shallots, sliced thinly
coriander leaves
fish sauce

Peel cucumber, slice in half lengthways and remove seeds with a spoon. Slice into 1 cm (½ inch) slices. Dissolve sugar in vinegar, and toss cucumber well in the mixture. Sprinkle over finely minced chilli, crushed peanuts, shallots and coriander leaves. Marinate for 1 hour.

Sprinkle with a dash of fish sauce before serving.

GAENG KEO WAN GAI
CHICKEN CURRY

1 no. 20 chicken (4 lbs)
20 ml (1 tablespoon) green curry paste (see glossary)
20 ml (1 tablespoon) vegetable oil
2 stalks lemon grass, tender part only
2 plants coriander, root and stalk, chopped
750 ml (3 cups) coconut milk
2–3 green chillis, seeded and chopped
1 cup basil leaves
20 ml (1 tablespoon) fish sauce

Remove skin from chicken and reserve for later use. Cut meat from bone and into strips. Fry curry paste in vegetable oil over a high flame for 2 minutes. Crush lemon grass and cut into 5 cm (2 inch) lengths and add to curry paste. Add coconut milk and cook until thick. Mix in chicken, chillis, coriander root and stalk and simmer for 15 minutes.

Before serving add basil leaves and fish sauce. Garnish with remaining coriander leaves.

HOMOK PLA
STEAMED FISH PUDDING

500 g (1 lb) white fish fillets
5 ml (1 teaspoon) Paste for Fish Pudding (see glossary)
500 ml (2 cups) coconut milk or cream
1 egg white
20 ml (1 tablespoon) fish sauce
10 shredded lettuce leaves
basil leaves or Kaffir lime leaves (Makrut)

Slice fish finely. Skim coconut cream from top of milk and reserve 40 ml
(2 tablespoons) for later use. Place fish in a bowl with curry paste. Stir in
coconut milk to dissolve the paste. Add egg white.

Stir pudding well by hand. The longer you stir the better the pudding. Mix
to a smooth paste. The secret is to leave a flaky fish texture in the pudding.
While stirring add fish sauce.

Line small steam baskets with lettuce and fill with fish mixture. Top each
basket with a teaspoon of coconut cream, a lime or basil leaf and a few
strips of red chilli.

Set small baskets into a bigger steamer and cook for 20 to 30 minutes
until fish is firm.

KAO HORM MALI
STEAMED FRAGRANT RICE

See recipe in glossary.

Homok Pla: Steamed fish pudding.

KAO NIEO MAMUANG
MANGOES WITH STICKY RICE

200 g (6½ oz) glutinous (sweet or sticky) rice
400 ml (1½ cup) thick coconut milk
pinch salt
100 ml (5 tablespoons) sugar syrup
6 or more mangoes
toasted sesame seeds

Wash rice well in running water, then soak in cold water overnight. Strain rice in a colander, and place in a steamer, cover and cook for 45 minutes. Remove and allow to cool.

Skim top of coconut milk and remove 100 ml of cream. Keep aside to finish dish. Add remaining coconut milk to cooled rice, with dissolved pinch of salt. Add sugar syrup. There is no need to chill rice if you are using it on the same day.

Peel required number of mangoes, one for each person. Slice each horizontally to the seed and arrange neatly on plate. Heap a small mound of rice next to sliced mango. Top with a teaspoon of reserved coconut cream and sprinkle with toasted sesame seeds.

Kao Nieo Mamuang: Mangoes with sticky rice.

DINNER AT RIM NAM

From the boat landing at the end of Oriental Avenue in Bangkok the East Asiatic Company buildings are on the left, and on the right,the original part of the Oriental Hotel, now more than 100 years old. The adjoining new part of the hotel is set in the most beautiful tropical gardens along the 'River of Kings'.

There is nothing to rival sitting on the riverside terrace with an exotic drink, watching the sun set behind the Temple of Dawn. The river is wide and fast-moving; a hub of activity with barges, boats and water-taxis constantly passing by. When I stay at the Oriental I feel as though I never want to leave. The gardens are so lush and cool, the pools so luxurious and the restaurants so splendid, that one could live there forever.

Crossing the Chao Phya River in a water-taxi from the Oriental Hotel landing is an adventure during monsoon when seasonal tides flood its banks. After an exhilarating ride across the swirling waters, guests are welcomed at *Rim Nam*, a Thai restaurant, with a façade resembling an old temple. Rim Nam means a water's edge, and from the terrace of the restaurant, dining in the moonlight is an exotic experience.

Bougainvillea grows in giant urns, trailing showers of brilliantly coloured blossoms, purple and fiery red. A porcelain balustrade encloses the terrace which is softly lit by old cast-iron carriage lamps.

I first tasted the 'burned' eggplant salad at a friend's suggestion and it soon became a favourite of mine. In Thai markets it is always possible to buy candle corn or baby corn in little bundles. Their texture is crisp and fresh, and an ideal contrast to chicken.

Although not as hot as a traditional Thai curry, Musaman beef curry has an overtone of Sudran spices; the Indian influence. The origin of the dish is with the Muslim settlers in the south of Thailand.

Tom Yam Goong is one of the most popular dishes to be served at a Thai table. As it stands in a charcoal-heated steamboat the flavour improves throughout your meal.

Pumpkin filled with coconut custard is a blend of simple ingredients, tempting to the palate and appealing to the eye.

YAM MAKEUA PAW
EGGPLANT SALAD

GAI PAD KAO POD ORN
CHICKEN WITH BABY CORN

GAENG MUSAMAN NEUA
MUSAMAN BEEF CURRY

TOM YAM GOONG
SOUR PRAWN SOUP

KAO HORM MALI
STEAMED FRAGRANT RICE

SANKAYA FAK THONG
COCONUT PUMPKIN CUSTARD

YAM MAKEUA PAW
EGGPLANT SALAD

3 eggplants, long green ones are best
100 g (4 oz) dried shrimps
40 ml (2 tablespoons) lime juice
40 ml (2 tablespoons) fish sauce
3 red chillis, chopped

Roast eggplant over a gas flame in a small wire dish, or grill under broiler, turning from time to time. The skin will be charred and the flesh inside will be soft.

Carefully remove eggplant skin and place soft flesh in a bowl. Place dried shrimps in food processor and blend until fine and floss-like. Mix lime juice, fish sauce and chillis together. Pour over warm eggplant, stir lightly and sprinkle with dried shrimp floss. Cooking time will be 7–15 minutes depending on thickness of eggplant and heat source.

GAI PAD KAO POD ORN
CHICKEN WITH BABY CORN

4 chicken breasts, removed from bone
30 ml (1 ½ tablespoons) oil for frying
4 cloves garlic, sliced finely
1 capsicum, cut into strips
2 chillis, cut into strips
250 g (8 oz) candle corn or baby corn
20 ml (1 tablespoon) fish sauce
20 ml (1 tablespoon) soy sauce

Cut chicken into strips. Heat oil in a wok and stir-fry chicken to seal, for 2 to 3 minutes. Remove to a platter.

In remaining oil fry garlic until golden brown. Add capsicum and chillis, quickly stir-fry. Return chicken to wok, stirring with vegetables. Add fish and soy sauce. Toss to blend well together. Serve on heated platter.

GAENG MUSAMAN NEUA
MUSAMAN BEEF CURRY

1 kg (2 lbs) topside beef, cut into 5 cm (2 inch) squares
40 ml (2 tablespoons) vegetable oil for frying
500 g (1 lb) small pickling onions, whole
500 g (1 lb) small new potatoes
40 ml (2 tablespoons) Musaman curry paste (see below)
1 litre (4 cups) coconut milk
125 ml (½ cup) tamarind water (mak kam) (see glossary)
6 cardamom pods
3 bay leaves
75 g (3 tablespoons) brown sugar

MUSAMAN CURRY PASTE

½ cup shallots (red onions)
½ cup garlic, chopped
½ cup lemon grass, tender parts only, chopped
20 peppercorns
15–20 dried red chillis
1 tablespoon coriander seeds, roasted
1 tablespoon cumin seeds, roasted
½ teaspoon nutmeg, freshly grated
½ teaspoon cloves
3 cardamom pods, roasted
2 tablespoons shrimp paste (kapee)

To make paste:

Place all spices on a sheet of foil and roast in the oven at 150°C (300°F) for 10 minutes. This releases the fragrance. Pound all above ingredients in mortar and pestle or blend in a food processor. Store in a closed glass jar in refrigerator until required.

To make curry:

Heat oil in a heavy based saucepan over a high flame and brown beef to seal. Remove and set aside. Fry onions and potatoes until brown, and reserve. Fry curry paste until fragrant, about 2 minutes, add coconut milk, and tamarind water. Boil for 15 minutes until thickened.

Add beef, onions and potatoes to curry mixture with cardamom, bay leaves and sugar. Simmer over low flame until potatoes are cooked, about 30 minutes.

TOM YAM GOONG
SOUR PRAWN SOUP

8 large prawns or 16 small prawns
2 litres (8 cups) water
3 stalks lemon grass, tender part only
5 Makrut or Kaffir lime leaves
150 g (5 oz) small mushroom caps or straw mushrooms
40 ml (2 tablespoons) fish sauce
4–6 fresh chillis, crushed
4 spring onions, cut into 2½ cm (1 inch) pieces
100 ml (5 tablespoons) fresh lime juice
10 ml (2 teaspoons) chilli paste
1 cup coriander leaves

Clean and devein prawns, leaving head and tail intact. Crush and slice lemon grass in 5 cm (2 inch) pieces. Bring water to boil in a large pot and add lemon grass, lime leaves, mushrooms, whole or sliced in half, fish sauce, and chillis. Boil for 2 minutes then add remaining ingredients. Cook only until prawns turn pink. Toss in coriander leaves before serving.

KAO HORM MALI
STEAMED FRAGRANT RICE

See recipe in glossary.

SANKAYA FAK THONG
COCONUT CUSTARD IN A PUMPKIN

1.5 kg (3 lbs) pumpkin, well coloured and shaped
custard
4 large eggs
100 g (3½ oz) raw sugar
200 ml (¾ cup) coconut cream

Prepare pumpkin by washing and drying outer skin. Cut out stem with a small knife, and retain to use as a lid. Do not make opening too large; it will affect custard filling and final slicing when chilled. Spoon out fibre and seeds. Place pumpkin upside down in a steam basket and steam for 15 minutes to partly cook flesh.

To make custard:

Place eggs in a bowl and whisk with sugar. Add coconut milk and stir until warm in double boiler. Pour warm custard into partly cooked pumpkin and cover with stem lid. Standing upright, steam again for 45 minutes, until custard is set and pumpkin is tender. Test with skewer through pumpkin skin. Remove steam basket from heat and allow to cool.

   Place pumpkin carefully on platter and chill well in refrigerator overnight. Slice in segments to serve.

PATTAYA DINNER

In 1964 I was involved with the development of the first major beach resort at Pattaya, 148 kilometres south-east of Bangkok. Nipa Lodge was the first hotel on a fabulous beach between two sleepy fishing villages.

A fishing boat would take us to a beautiful coral island, just one hour off-shore and we caught fish on the way. Now Pattaya has become a tourist destination for sun-seekers from all over the world.

In the warm Thai waters there is a small indigenous fish called Pla Too which, unfortunately, is not found anywhere else in the world. It is an important part of Thai cuisine and is sold ready to eat. It can be smoked then toasted over a charcoal fire, or steamed in a bamboo basket.

Visiting the markets in Pattaya is an experience for all who enjoy seafood. Stalls are laden with glistening fresh fish from the Gulf waters. Shellfish, including succulent lobster, fresh from the fishing boats, are ready at daybreak in the bustling markets.

Fresh sardines are a good substitute for Pla Too. I like to use Spanish mackerel, sliced thinly into cutlets and crisp-fried. Cooked this way, it is easier to remove skin and bones from the fish.

Snow peas are versatile and quick to prepare; their texture crisp and crunchy. Lobster curry, flavoured with Chinese dates, has a sweet and sour finish, coloured a delicate pink.

Pumpkin combined with coconut milk and dried shrimps can be used as a base for any variation. Add some fish wings (often the most tasty part) or cooked chicken pieces.

Pomelo, one of the great fruits of Asia, has a thick rind with pinkish-yellow coloured segments. It resembles a grapefruit in both size and colour, but has a more juicy definite texture. Its taste sensation and texture makes the pomelo a perfect choice to end a Pattaya seafood dinner.

MIANG PLA TOO
SALAD OF SARDINES OR MACKEREL

GAENG KAREE GOONG
LOBSTER CURRY

THUA LANDAU NAMMAN HOIE
SNOW PEAS WITH GARLIC AND OYSTER SAUCE

GAENG LIENG FAK THONG
PUMPKIN AND COCONUT SOUP

KAO HORM MALI
STEAMED FRAGRANT RICE

SOM-OR CHAE
CHILLED POMELO SEGMENTS

MIANG PLA TOO
SALAD OF SARDINES OR MACKEREL

1 kg (2 lbs) sardines or
    750 g (1½ lbs) mackerel cutlets
80 ml (4 tablespoons) peanut or vegetable oil
4–6 shallots (red onions)
3 cm (1 inch) fresh ginger
2–4 red chillis
2–4 green chillis
100 g (4 oz) raw, toasted peanuts, skins removed
1 green mango
50 ml (2 tablespoons) fresh lime juice
1 teaspoon fresh lime zest, grated
40 ml (2 tablespoons) fish sauce
lettuce leaves, mignonette or butter crunch
coriander leaves

Clean sardines or mackerel cutlets and pat dry. Fry in hot oil and drain well.
Remove skin and bones from fish. Place cleaned fish in a bowl.

Finely slice shallots. Peel ginger and chop finely. Slice all chillis finely.
Roast peanuts in oven on medium heat for 10 minutes to loosen skins. Rub
between a kitchen towel to remove skins. Crush nuts finely. Peel skin from
mango, chop or dice fruit. Place these ingredients in the bowl with fish.
Toss lime juice and zest with fish sauce through the mixture carefully to
avoid breaking fish.

Pile on to a serving platter. Arrange chilled lettuce leaves around fish and
garnish with coriander leaves. The salad is spooned into lettuce leaves,
rolled up and eaten.

GAENG KAREE GOONG
LOBSTER CURRY

4 lobster tails or 8 large prawns
80 ml (4 tablespoons) vegetable oil
30 g (1 tablespoon) red curry paste
1 red capsicum, diced finely
2 red chillis, chopped finely
20 ml fish sauce
25 g (1 tablespoon) sugar
500 ml (2 cups) coconut milk
16 dried Chinese dates
fresh coriander leaves to garnish

Remove lobster meat from shells and cut into bite-size pieces. If using prawns, peel and devein, leaving head and tail intact. Heat vegetable oil in a wok, add lobster meat or prawns and stir-fry for 3 to 4 minutes, until meat is just cooked. Remove lobster or prawns and reserve.

Add curry paste, stirring quickly until fragrant. Toss in capsicum and chillis, add fish sauce, sugar, coconut milk and dried dates. Stir well and reduce heat to simmer. Allow to thicken, around 5 minutes.

Return lobster or prawns, warm through quickly. Serve garnished with coriander leaves.

THUA LANDAU NAMMAN HOIE
SNOW PEAS WITH GARLIC AND OYSTER SAUCE

500 g (1 lb) snow peas
30 ml (1½ tablespoons) vegetable oil
3 cloves of garlic, thinly sliced
3 spring onions, sliced
40 ml (1 tablespoon) oyster sauce
10 ml (2 teaspoons) fish sauce
1 teaspoon sugar

Wash and string snow peas. Heat oil in a wok and fry garlic until golden. Add snow peas and spring onions tossing quickly. Add oyster sauce, fish sauce and sugar. Stir quickly. Cooking should take no more than 2 minutes.

GAENG LIENG FAK THONG
PUMPKIN AND COCONUT SOUP

1 kg (2 lbs) pumpkin
2 tablespoons fresh lime juice
150 g (5 oz) dried shrimps
4 shallots (red onions) chopped
4–6 red chillis, chopped
1 stalk lemon grass, tender part only, chopped
800 ml (3 cups) coconut milk
2 tablespoons shrimp paste
300 ml (1½ cups) tamarind water (see glossary)
1 litre fish stock, chicken stock or water
20 ml (1 tablespoon) fish sauce
1 bunch basil

Peel pumpkin, removing seeds and fibre. Dice, place in bowl and sprinkle with lime juice. Leave to stand while preparing other ingredients.

Mix dried shrimps, shallots, chillis and lemon grass in food processor and blend to a fine paste. Skim cream from coconut milk and reserve. Add contents of food processor bowl, shrimp paste and coconut milk to a large saucepan. Stir until dissolved. Bring to boil, add tamarind water and simmer for 10 minutes. Add pumpkin pieces and cook until tender. Add stock or water and return to boil. Season with fish sauce.

Before serving stir in coconut cream and basil leaves.

KAO HORM MALI
STEAMED FRAGRANT RICE

See recipe in glossary.

SOM-OR CHAE
CHILLED POMELO SEGMENTS

Use 2 pomelo for 8 persons

Peel thick skin from the fruit. Remove white pith and carefully pull segments apart. Try to keep segments whole. The next tedious step is to remove all fibrous membrane from each segment. Chill before serving.

DINNER IN THE ORCHARD

On a visit to the country, a friend found an old wooden Thai house and had it moved to Thonburi, across the river from Bangkok. The houses along the klongs (canals), where most people lived, were built high on stilts. His house was moved to a durian orchard, criss-crossed by canals. It was fun to ride in a longtailed boat and arrive for dinner.

We sat on a straw mat on the verandah overlooking the orchard and were served this wonderful feast.

A huge pot of mussels cooked with lemon grass was placed in the middle. We picked up the mussels with our fingers and dipped them into a mixture of lime juice, fish sauce and chopped chillis and washed them down with Mekong whiskey and soda, spiked with a slice of lime.

Then came a bamboo steamer filled with pearly rice-covered meatballs. Although not strictly Thai, they are a delicate addition to any menu.

The green papaya salad, served on an antique celadon plate, was a perfect blending of subtle colours and flavours.

The cook proudly brought us a platter holding a red snapper, crisply fried, covered with a gleaming white chilli sauce and a silver bowl of steaming fragrant rice.

We all helped ourselves to a succulent mussel, a pearly meatball, then a taste of spicy fish, a spoonful of papaya salad, then cooling rice. With food served this way, it is possible to rotate taste sensations at will. It is the essence of a Thai meal.

To finish the maid produced a home-churned ice-cream similar to my own recipe for sweet potato ice-cream.

HOIE MAN POO
MUSSELS WITH LEMON GRASS

LOOK MOO DOON
PEARLY MEATBALLS

SOM TUM
GREEN PAPAYA SALAD

PLA KHOW LARD PRIK
CRISP FRIED SNAPPER OR RED EMPEROR
WITH CHILLI SAUCE

KAO HORM MALI
STEAMED FRAGRANT RICE

SWEET POTATO ICE-CREAM

HOIE MAN POO
MUSSELS WITH LEMON GRASS

3 kg (6 lbs) fresh mussels in their shells
60 ml (3 tablespoons) peanut or vegetable oil
3 onions, chopped finely
3 cloves garlic, crushed
3 red chillis, chopped
3 stalks lemon grass, tender part only, crushed
250 ml (1 cup) dry white wine
1 bunch (1 cup) basil leaves

Clean mussels under cold running water. Remove fibre and beard, discarding any open shells. Heat oil in a large saucepan, and sauté onions, garlic and chillis for 2 minutes until soft but not coloured. Add lemon grass and wine, simmer for 5 minutes. Add cleaned mussels and half the basil leaves. Cover pan with lid and cook over a high flame for 10 minutes. The mussels will have opened and are then cooked.

Serve mussels in individual bowls, pour over stock and garnish with remaining basil leaves.

LOOK MOO DOON
PEARLY MEATBALLS

500 g (1 lb) minced lean pork, loin or fillet
2.5 cm (1 inch) fresh ginger
10 water chestnuts, chopped
2 spring onions, chopped
2 egg yolks
1 whole egg
salt and pepper to taste
500 g (1 lb) long grain rice
soy sauce to serve

Rinse rice and soak in cold water for 2 to 3 hours, drain and dry on a kitchen towel. Mix minced pork with all other ingredients to form a farce. Allow to stand for 1 hour.

Yam Goong: Salad of slipper lobster with mint and lemon grass.

Shape mixture into bite-size balls and roll in rice to completely cover. Place meatballs in a steamer basket over boiling water. Steam for 20 to 30 minutes until rice is cooked.

Serve with soy sauce flavoured with sake or dry sherry; one part sake to one of soy sauce.

SOM TUM
GREEN PAPAYA SALAD

1 small green papaya or pawpaw
100 g snake beans or string beans
200 g (7 oz) cooked chicken meat, cut into strips
2 red chillis
2 green chillis
75 ml (4 tablespoons) fresh lime juice
20 ml (1 tablespoon) fish sauce
50 g (2 tablespoons) brown sugar or palm sugar
1 clove garlic, finely chopped
2.5 cm (1 inch) fresh ginger, finely chopped
25 g (1 oz) dried shrimps, finely chopped in food
   processor, to garnish
25 g (1 oz) roasted peanuts, finely chopped

Peel and seed papaya. Finely slice the fruit. Crush beans with a knife, cut into 5 cm (2 inch) lengths and place in bowl with papaya. Add chicken.

Finely chop one red and one green chilli. Combine lime juice, fish sauce and sugar, stirring until dissolved. Add to chopped chillis, garlic, ginger and toss well with chicken and papaya.

Serve on a platter sprinkled with shrimp floss, chopped peanuts and garnished with remaining chillis, sliced.

Above: Tord Man Pla: Fried fish cakes. Middle: Yam Thaeng Kwa: Spiced cucumber salad. Below: Pla Muek Kratiem Prik Thai: Squid with fresh green peppercorns.

PLA KHOW LARD PRIK
CRISP FRIED SNAPPER OR RED EMPEROR
WITH CHILLI SAUCE

1 kg whole snapper or red emperor, scaled and gutted
3 red chillis, chopped
3 green chillis, chopped
2 cm (¾ inch) fresh ginger, chopped
3 shallots (red onions), chopped
2 cloves garlic, chopped
10 white peppercorns or fresh green peppercorns
20 ml (1 tablespoon) coriander roots, chopped
100 ml (5 tablespoons) vegetable oil
20 ml (1 tablespoon) fish sauce
60 ml (3 tablespoons) tamarind water (see glossary)
60 g (2 tablespoons) brown sugar
250 ml (1 cup) thick coconut milk
coriander leaves

Score fish along the sides, trim fins leaving head and tail intact. Mix chillis, ginger, shallots, garlic, peppercorns and coriander to a fine paste. Heat oil in a wok or frying pan, and cook fish until crisp and golden. Drain on paper towels and keep warm on a serving dish.

Pour off most of the oil from pan, add paste and stir-fry for 2 minutes. Add fish sauce, tamarind water and sugar. Simmer for 3 minutes, add coconut milk, bring to boil and simmer for 5 minutes.

Pour sauce over fish and garnish with coriander leaves.

KAO HORM MALI
STEAMED FRAGRANT RICE

See recipe in glossary.

SWEET POTATO ICE-CREAM

3 sweet potatoes, orange
300 g (1 cup) raw sugar
1 whole egg
250 ml (1 cup) milk
750 ml (3 cups) whipped cream
40 ml (2 tablespoons) white rum

Peel sweet potatoes. Steam until soft, about 20 minutes. Cut into pieces and blend until smooth in a food processor. Add sugar, egg and milk, mixing well.

Place mixture in a bowl and stand over ice to cool. When cold, whip cream and fold in gently, adding rum. Turn into ice-cream maker, churn and freeze.

LUNCH AT SONGKLA

Often, I used to take an overnight boat trip across the Gulf of Thailand to Samui Island. Another day's boat ride would bring me to Songkla, a resort on the coast, halfway down the Gulf. The Samila Hotel on the peninsula outside Songkla was a splendid place in which to relax. From one side of the peninsula the view swept down to the South China Sea. The view from the other side overlooked Lake Songkla, which flowed to the sea.

I lunched at the restaurant near the hotel, which had tables and chairs set on the sand underneath towering coconut palms over sixty years old. People came from all over the world to enjoy the tropical location and fresh seafood. Ice-cold Singha beer was served in frozen glass mugs, often with a lump of ice in the base.

Food was plentiful in this area, although mainly from the sea. Sweet and tender water buffalo was used in the Thai beef salad.

Mussels, straight from the sea, piled on larger shells were brightly garnished with red chillis and coriander. Stuffed mushrooms floated in the Chinese-style soup, with crunchy watermelon.

Sand crabs with their red shells glistening, served in coconut sauce, was a favourite local dish. Mud crabs and prawns are a perfect choice for this recipe. Local fishermen netted squid every night; small, pink and tender.

Small boys carried containers of coconut ice-cream over their shoulders; it was a treat, topped with crushed peanuts and eaten with a spoon. After each serving the boys would rinse the enamel cups and spoon in the clear blue sea.

YAM NEUA
THAI BEEF SALAD

HOMOK HOIE MAN POO
STEAMED STUFFED MUSSELS

GAENG CHUD
SOUP WITH STUFFED MUSHROOMS

BANANA PRAWNS AND MUDCRAB IN COCONUT SAUCE

PLA MUEK KRATIEM PRIK THAI
SQUID WITH FRESH GREEN PEPPERCORNS

KAO HORM MALI
STEAMED FRAGRANT RICE

ICE-CREAM KA TI
COCONUT ICE-CREAM

YAM NEUA
THAI BEEF SALAD

1 kg (2 lb) lean sirloin, rump or fillet
¼ cup coriander leaves, chopped
2 cloves garlic, chopped
40 ml (2 tablespoons) soy sauce
40 ml (2 tablespoons) fresh lime juice or lemon juice
20 ml (1 tablespoon) fish sauce
30 g (1 oz) brown sugar or palm sugar
2 shallots (red onions), thinly sliced
4 red fresh chillis, cut into strips
¼ cup fresh mint leaves
250 g (1 punnet) cherry tomatoes
lettuce leaves

Roast beef rare to medium. Leave to rest and cool.

Mix coriander leaves, garlic, soy sauce, lime juice, fish sauce and sugar in a food processor, blending to a smooth paste. Slice cooled beef as thin as possible. Toss in marinade paste with half the mint leaves.

Arrange lettuce leaves on a platter with slices of beef to one side. Garnish with shallots, chillis, cherry tomatoes and remaining mint leaves.

HOMOK HOIE MAN POO
STEAMED STUFFED MUSSELS

3 kg (6 lbs) fresh mussels in their shells
2 cups basil leaves
red chilli strips
coriander leaves

Stuffing

½ cup shallots (red onions), chopped
½ cup garlic, chopped
½ cup lemon grass, tender parts, chopped
3–6 fresh red chillis
2 tablespoons shrimp paste
40 ml (2 tablespoons) vegetable oil for frying

Paste

50 g (2 oz) rice flour
500 ml (2 cups) coconut cream

Mix all stuffing ingredients, except oil, in food processor to a smooth paste. Turn into hot oil and fry until fragrant, about 2 minutes. Mix together rice flour and coconut cream. Blend well together with processed ingredients. Set aside. Scrub mussels with a stiff brush under cold running water to remove sand and beard. Place in steamer, cover and cook over boiling water until shells open. Remove from heat and take mussels from shells. Reserve the larger and better looking shells.

Blanch basil leaves to soften. Place one leaf, on each shell, top with 2 or 3 mussels, then spoon paste over to cover. Garnish each shell with chilli strips. Return to steamer and heat through. Sprinkle with coriander leaves.

GAENG CHUD
SOUP WITH STUFFED MUSHROOMS

12 dried Chinese mushrooms
125 g (4 oz) lean pork, minced
2 water chestnuts, chopped
1 clove of garlic, chopped
2 shallots (red onions), chopped
1 teaspoon coriander root, chopped
1 teaspoon coriander leaves, chopped
2 teaspoons soy sauce
2 teaspoons sake or dry sherry
salt and pepper to taste
150 g (5 oz) watermelon
1.5 litres (6 cups) clear chicken stock
2 cloves garlic, thinly sliced and fried until crisp to garnish

Soak mushrooms in warm water for 40 minutes. Discard hard stems. Place minced pork in a bowl; add water chestnuts, garlic, shallots, coriander root and leaves, soy, sake and seasoning. Mix thoroughly, adding a little water to make a smooth paste. Fill mushroom caps with mixture and steam over boiling water for 20 minutes.

Cut watermelon in bite-size pieces or make melon balls. Bring stock to boil, add melon and cook for 10 minutes. Spoon melon in soup dishes, add stuffed mushrooms, and pour over hot stock. Garnish with crisp fried garlic.

BANANA PRAWNS AND MUD CRAB IN COCONUT SAUCE

1 kg (2 lb) green banana or tiger prawns
1 kg (2 lb) cooked crab
2 cloves garlic, chopped
1 tablespoon vegetable oil
2 stalks lemon grass, crushed and cut into 3 mm (¼ inch) pieces
3 fresh red chillis, chopped
300 ml (1½ cups) coconut milk
coriander to garnish
shredded coconut to garnish

Sauté garlic in vegetable oil, add lemon grass and chillis. Pour in coconut milk, bring to boil and simmer over low heat for 4 minutes. Add prawns and toss well in sauce. Crack crab claws, add to mixture with crab meat. Mix well and cover to quickly heat through.

Serve garnished with coriander and shredded coconut.

PLA MUEK KRATIEM PRIK THAI
SQUID WITH FRESH GREEN PEPPERCORNS

750 g (24 oz) squid, cleaned and cut into rings
100 ml (5 tablespoons) cooking oil
4 cloves garlic, thinly sliced
40 ml (2 tablespoons) fresh green peppercorns or tinned
1 bunch (1 cup) fresh basil leaves
40 ml (2 tablespoons) fish sauce
40 ml (2 tablespoons) soy sauce

Heat oil in wok, stir-fry sliced garlic and add lightly crushed green peppercorns. Add squid and stir-fry for 3 minutes. Toss in basil leaves, adding fish sauce and soy sauce. Heat through quickly. Serve on a platter garnished with lemon slices.

KAO HORM MALI
STEAMED FRAGRANT RICE

See recipe in glossary.

ICE-CREAM KA TI
COCONUT ICE-CREAM

1 litre (4 cups) coconut milk
3 leaves gelatine or 2 teaspoons gelatine powder
150 g (6 oz) castor sugar
pinch salt
2 egg whites, lightly beaten

Soak gelatine in cold water. Warm coconut milk with sugar and salt. Add softened gelatine and mix thoroughly. Whisk in egg white. Turn into ice-cream maker, churn and freeze.

DINNER ON BOARD *PANU RANGSRI*

When I lived in Thailand one of my favourite trips was to board a coastal liner, *Panu Rangsri*, in the middle of the river outside the Oriental Hotel. By early evening we would be slowly winding our way out of Bangkok to the open water, heading south in the Gulf of Thailand. I would get off at an island called Kho Samui and spend a week painting before joining the boat on its return trip to Bangkok.

Although there were never more than four passengers, the dinner served on board was fresh and good. Chicken wrapped in pandanus leaves came as a starter with a delicious nutty flavour. On the table there would be a large steaming bowl of curried mussels and a platter of colourful pickled vegetables. Beef was quickly stir-fried with oyster sauce and served with a bowl of fragrant steamed rice.

The versatile wing bean came in a salad with prawns and chicken. It is a useful bean to have growing in the garden; the leaves can be cooked as spinach, the bean served as a cooked vegetable or in a salad garnished with its flowers, and the tuber is a source of protein. The coffee and coconut jelly is typical of Thai sweets using agar agar, cooling the palate at the end of a meal.

It was a relaxed evening with the captain offering endless whiskeys throughout the dinner. The chief engineer had worked on the boat since it first came to Thailand in 1928. He was proud of his immaculate engine room with highly polished brass and copper fittings. For two nights I would sleep on deck under the stars. Early in the morning longtailed boats would come alongside to collect passengers and supplies. Sometimes the wind was so strong, we had to jump into the small boat rolling in the sea. Once safely on the boat and heading to shore, our arrival on the island was sheer heaven.

GAI OB BAI TOEY
CHICKEN IN PANDANUS LEAVES

YAM TUA POO
WING BEAN SALAD

GAENG HOIE MAN POO
CURRIED MUSSELS

PAK DONG
PICKLED VEGETABLES

NEUA PAD NAMMAN HOIE
BEEF WITH OYSTER SAUCE

KAO HORM MALI
STEAMED FRAGRANT RICE

KANOM THAI
COFFEE AND COCONUT JELLY

GAI OB BAI TOEY
CHICKEN IN PANDANUS LEAVES

1 kg (2 lbs) chicken meat with skin removed
2 shallots (red onions), chopped
2 cloves garlic, chopped
2 cm (¾ inch) fresh ginger, peeled and chopped
1 tablespoon coriander root, chopped
1 tablespoon lemon grass, tender part only, chopped
20 ml (1 tablespoon) fish sauce
20 ml (1 tablespoon) soy sauce
20 ml (1 tablespoon) worcestershire sauce
26 g (1 tablespoon) brown sugar
250 ml (1 cup) thick coconut milk
fresh ground pepper
oil for frying
coriander leaves
pandanus leaves or banana leaves

Cut chicken in bite-size pieces and place in bowl. Mix together shallots, garlic, ginger, coriander root, lemon grass, fish, soy and worcestershire sauces, sugar, coconut milk and blend in food processor. Pour marinade over chicken, mix well to cover and allow to stand for 30 minutes.

Wrap each piece of chicken in a pandanus leaf and secure with a toothpick. Heat oil in wok and cook wrapped chicken pieces until tender, about 10 minutes. Serve at the beginning of a meal.

YAM TUA POO
WING BEAN SALAD

500 g wing beans
250 g (½ lb) cooked chicken meat
250 g (½ lb) cooked prawns, shelled, tail intact
30 g (2 tablespoons) garlic, sliced
30 g (2 tablespoons) shallots (red onions), chopped
10 g (1 tablespoon) dried chillis
40 g (2 tablespoons) chilli paste
50 ml (3 tablespoons) fresh lime juice
125 ml (½ cup) coconut cream

25 g (1 tablespoon) sugar
40 g (2 tablespoons) roasted peanuts, crushed
40 g (2 tablespoons) roasted coconut

Slice wing beans thinly across and blanch quickly in boiling water. Strain and refresh in ice water to retain colour. Place in a bowl with chicken cut into strips. Slice garlic and shallots thinly. Fry chillis in a little oil to crisp, then crush with the side of a knife.

To make dressing:

Dissolve chilli paste in lime juice, adding coconut cream and sugar. Pour over prawns, chicken and beans.

Toss well with chillis, garlic, shallots, peanuts and coconut. Serve at room temperature.

GAENG HOIE MAN POO
CURRIED MUSSELS

3 kg (6 lbs) mussels in shells, makes 1 kg (2 lbs) when removed from shells
1½ tablespoons red curry paste (see glossary)
100 ml (2 cups) coconut milk
20 ml (1 tablespoon) fish sauce
20 ml (1 tablespoon) raw or brown sugar
150 g (5 oz) straw mushrooms or button mushrooms
5–6 fresh red chillies
½ cup basil leaves

Clean mussels under cold running water with a stiff brush to remove sand and beard. Steam in a bamboo basket over boiling water, covered, for 30 seconds to open. Remove mussels from their shells and reserve.

Heat wok to medium, add curry paste and cook until fragrant. Add a little coconut milk and stir until paste has dissolved. Add fish sauce, sugar and remaining coconut milk, cooking until sauce has thickened. Toss in mushrooms, chillis and basil leaves, cooking for 1 minute. Add mussels and warm through. Remove to a serving platter.

PAK DONG
PICKLED VEGETABLES

250 g (10 oz) cauliflower
250 g (10 oz) small cucumbers
250 g (10 oz) cabbage
250 g (10 oz) baby corn or corn kernels
500 ml (2 cups) white vinegar
50 g (2 tablespoons) salt
2 shallots (red onions), chopped
4 fresh red chillis, chopped
2 cloves garlic, chopped
250 ml (1 cup) peanut oil
25 g (1 oz) toasted sesame seeds to garnish
coriander leaves to garnish

Trim and cut all vegetables into bite-size pieces. Bring vinegar to boil with salt and blanch vegetables for 1 minute.

Mix together shallots, chopped chillis and garlic in a food processor to form a smooth paste. Heat peanut oil and fry paste for one minute. Toss in blanched vegetables and stir-fry for a few seconds. Remove to a bowl. Garnish with toasted sesame seeds and a few sprigs of coriander leaves.

Pickled vegetables can be refrigerated in a glass jar for a week.

NEUA PAD NAMMAN HOIE
BEEF WITH OYSTER SAUCE

500 g (1 lb) sirloin or tenderloin of beef
40 ml (2 tablespoons) vegetable oil
4 cloves garlic, thinly sliced
40 ml (2 tablespoons) oyster sauce
40 ml (2 tablespoons) fish sauce
10 shallots, cut into 5 cm (2 inch) pieces
10 ml (2 tablespoons) sugar
fresh ground pepper to taste

Slice beef thinly across grain. Heat oil in wok until hot and stir-fry beef quickly to colour. Remove and reserve. Add garlic and stir-fry until golden. Add oyster sauce, fish sauce, shallots, sugar and pepper. Return beef to wok and coat with sauce. Serve at once.

KAO HORM MALI
STEAMED FRAGRANT RICE

See recipe in glossary.

KANOM THAI
COFFEE AND COCONUT JELLY

10 g (⅓ oz) agar agar
500 ml (2 cups) coconut milk
2 teaspoons instant coffee
500 ml (2 cups) water, boiling
60 g (2 oz) brown sugar

Dissolve half the quantity of agar agar in warm coconut milk, stirring well. Pour into a jelly mould, set over ice or in refrigerator until firm. The mould should be half-full only. Dissolve instant coffee in boiling water, add remaining 5 g agar agar and sugar. Stir well to dissolve and set aside to cool. When coconut jelly has set, pour cool coffee-flavoured jelly over the top, to fill jelly mould. Refrigerate overnight.

   To serve, turn out jelly from mould. There will be two contrasting colours; the coconut jelly over coffee jelly. This is a palate-cooling dessert to serve after a spicy meal.

KATHIN LUNCH

At the end of the Buddhist lent, Kathin, is the traditional time for people to present new robes to the monks at their temple. At the same time, the King travels by boat down the river with new robes for the priest at Wat Arun, 'The Temple of Dawn'.

The King's boat called 'Suwannahong', is made from carved, gilded wood, 45 metres long and 3 metres wide. On board are fifty-eight men, fifty of whom are oarsmen in spectacular, colourful uniforms. Following the King's boat is a flotilla of thirty-five more boats, each opulently decorated.

I was invited by naval friends to watch the spectacle from their house on the river. It proved to be a perfect vantage point.

While we waited lunch was served; the dishes were a combination I had not tried before.

Ice-cold rice, called khao chae, is scented with jasmine flowers and served in small dishes. In the early days of Thailand, ice was imported by boat from Singapore for the royal court.

Peppers and pumpkin flowers are stuffed with farce, dipped in batter, crisp fried and served right away. Long beans, strips of eggplant, spring onions with their tops left on are delicious cooked in this crunchy batter.

Coconut pancakes, kanom kluk, are cooked in a cast-iron pan with indentations, a traditional Thai utensil. The pancakes can be topped with a savoury mixture for serving with cocktails, or with a sweet topping for dessert or snack with tea.

Gaeng Musaman Neua: Beef Musaman.
Gaeng Kheo Wan Gai: Chicken curry.

KHAO CHAE
ICED RICE

NEUA WAN
SWEET CRISP BEEF

PRIK YUAK SAI
STUFFED PEPPERS

STUFFED PUMPKIN FLOWERS

SNAKE BEANS, EGGPLANT, SPRING ONIONS IN BATTER

KANOM KLUK
COCONUT PANCAKES

NAM MANAO
LIMEADE

Tom Yam Goong: Sour prawn soup.

KHAO CHAE
ICED RICE

600 g (2 cups) long grain Thai rice

Soak rice for 2 to 3 hours. Wash in plenty of cold water to remove starch. Bring rice to boil and simmer for 5 minutes. Strain and wash. Bring to boil again and simmer for 5 minutes. Rinse and strain, repeating simmering process for another 5 minutes. Rinse again in cold water. The rice should be cooked and shiny. Set aside until ready to serve.

Place in small bowls with crushed ice and add cold jasmine water. Add 5 drops jasmine essence to 1 litre iced water.

NEUA WAN
SWEET CRISP BEEF

500 g (1 lb) sliced corn beef or silverside
250 ml (1 cup) vegetable oil
6 shallots (red onions), sliced thinly
4 cloves garlic, sliced thinly
sugar

Fry shallot slices in a little hot oil until crisp. Strain and keep to one side. In the same oil fry garlic slices until crisp, strain and put aside.

Slice beef into long thin strips. Heat more oil in wok and fry beef strips until almost dry, adding a handful of sugar. Continue to stir-fry until beef is crisp. Remove and drain on paper towels. Toss crisp beef with shallots and garlic.

PRIK YUAK SAI
STUFFED PEPPERS
STUFFED PUMPKIN FLOWERS
SNAKE BEANS, EGGPLANT, SPRING ONIONS
IN BATTER

12–20 small bell peppers, capsicum, or banana peppers
2 cloves garlic, chopped
10 peppercorns
2 shallots (red onions), chopped
3 coriander roots and stalks, chopped
oil for frying
250 g (½ lb) minced pork
250 g (½ lb) prawn meat, chopped
20 ml (1 tablespoon) fish sauce
25 g (1 tablespoon) sugar
1 egg
40 g (2 tablespoons) ground peanuts, roasted

Batter:

150 g (1 cup) plain flour
200 ml (¾ cup) water
1 teaspoon baking powder
pinch of salt and sugar
40 ml (2 tablespoons) vegetable oil

Using whichever peppers are available, cut out stalk with a small knife and remove seeds. Pound garlic, peppercorns, shallots, coriander root and stalk or blend in food processor. Fry paste in a little hot oil, adding minced pork and prawn meat. Stir while cooking and add fish sauce and sugar. When cool remove to a bowl, bind with egg and add peanuts.

Fill prepared peppers leaving room for stuffing to expand, about two-thirds full. Keep to one side until ready to cook in batter when the meal is to be served. Dip into batter mix and deep fry until golden brown. Drain on paper towels.

To make batter:

Mix all batter ingredients together, blending well. This batter is simple and easy for any choice of vegetable.

Pumpkin flowers can also be stuffed with this mixture and deep fried until crisp.

For this lunch I suggest snake beans, eggplant strips and spring onions are dipped in batter and deep fried until golden and crisp.

KANOM KLUK
COCONUT PANCAKES

140 g (1 cup) rice flour
410 ml (1¾ cup) coconut milk
1 whole egg
pinch salt and sugar

In a Thai kitchen, the pan for cooking Kanom Kluk comes with little clay tops to cover each mould.

Whisk all ingredients in a bowl to make a smooth batter. Place cast-iron pan over a low flame and allow to heat through. Grease each indentation with clarified butter. When pan is hot fill each mould to the top and leave to bake slowly. To speed up this process, place the pan in a hot oven for a few minutes until the pancakes are cooked. They will turn golden on the underside while the top is just set. Remove to a serving dish and cook remaining batter in the same way.

Suggested toppings: dried shrimp floss mixed with chopped chives, chopped peanuts and dried chilli flakes; finely diced pumpkin, 'golden silk' (see Songkran Dinner), shredded coconut.

NAM MANAO
LIMEADE

6–10 fresh limes
120 g (4 oz) sugar
1 litre (4 cups) boiling water
pinch of salt

To make fresh limes easier to squeeze, roll on a table applying pressure with the palm of your hand. Squeeze juice and strain into a jug. Put lime rinds in a bowl with sugar and pour over boiling water. Allow to stand for no longer than 10 to 15 minutes. The hot water draws aromatic oil from lime rinds. Add infusion to fresh lime juice. Refrigerate until ready to use.

Fill a tall glass with ice cubes, add a few slices of lime, pour over chilled lime juice and top with sprigs of mint. A dash of soda or mineral water can be added but I prefer rainwater. It is a most refreshing drink and really popular in restaurants and hotels in Bangkok.

PICNIC LUNCH AT WANG TAKRAI

To escape the hot noisy city of Bangkok I often used to go with friends to the waterfalls of Salika, one hour's drive from the city. We would take a picnic to nearby Wang Takrai, the 'Lemon Grass Palace', and botanical gardens created by Prince and Princess Chumpot of Nagara Svarga. This wonderful retreat has 80 hectares of tropical rainforest, lush sweeping lawns and well-tended gardens. Visitors can use the resthouses and there are shelters around the gardens. One really hot day we arrived with our picnic, found a shelter and unpacked our lunch on to the table. A gardener turned on a tap at roof level and water cascaded over the sides creating a wonderful cooling atmosphere.

We had a large platter of fresh vegetables, intricately carved with a bowl of nam prik in the centre, to be used as a dip.

Portions of fried rice were wrapped in banana leaves. When opened they revealed a serving for each person.

Red pork, often seen hanging in a roadside food vendor's glass cabinet, ready for a quick stir-fried lunch, is delicious served cold. The thinly-sliced pork was arranged with small cucumber boats filled with marinated ginger, pickled garlic and salted hard boiled eggs in quarters.

We brought concentrated lime juice to make refreshing limeade from the crystal clear water of a mountain stream.

A friend had brought a container of chilled coconut cream with the meat of young coconut, thickened with seeds of sweet basil. We finished our picnic with fresh fruit found at a local market.

With my interest in gardening, there would always be something new in the gardens for me to see and learn about. After spending the afternoon in this cool lush setting we would drive back to Bangkok at sunset.

NAM PRIK
PLATTER OF RAW VEGETABLES WITH HOT CHILLI SAUCE

MOO DAENG
RED PORK

CUCUMBER BOATS

KHAO PHAD
FRIED RICE

NAM KATI SAI MED MANG LUCK
COCONUT MILK WITH SWEET BASIL SEEDS

TROPICAL FRUIT OF THE SEASON

NAM MANAO
LIMEADE

NAM PRIK
PLATTER OF RAW VEGETABLES WITH HOT CHILLI SAUCE

12 lettuce leaves
8 small white eggplant
2 young fennel, cut into 4–6 pieces
8 white or red cabbage leaves, carved
8 slices of green mango carved in the shape of leaves
8 broccoli flowerets
8 sticks of cucumber
8 green spring onions
8 snake or string beans
8 carrot slices, carved
8 small zucchini
8 capsicum strips, red, yellow and green
8 tiny cherry tomatoes
assorted crisp greens

NAM PRIK
HOT CHILLI SAUCE

3 cloves garlic, chopped
3 shallots (red onions), chopped
1 stalk lemon grass, chopped
6 fresh red chillis, chopped
1 tablespoon coriander root, chopped
25 g (1 tablespoon) shrimp paste
25 g (1 tablespoon) dried shrimps
25 g (1 tablespoon) brown sugar
80 ml (4 tablespoons) fish sauce
80 ml (4 tablespoons) fresh lime juice
10-20 bird's eye chillis, whole (prik e no suan)
10 pea eggplants (makeua puong), crushed and chopped

Chill vegetables well and serve arranged on a platter on a bed of ice. Place a bowl of nam prik in centre to be used as a dip.

To make chilli sauce (nam prik):

Heat garlic, shallots, lemon grass, chillis and coriander root in a skillet until they start to smoke. Place in a food processor bowl with shrimp paste, dried shrimps and brown sugar, adding fish sauce and lime juice. Blend to a smooth paste. Pour into a bowl. Add bird's eye chilli and eggplants to the sauce and float on top. Beware of whole chillis.

The sauce can be stored in jar for use as required.

MOO DAENG
RED PORK

1 kg (2 lbs) loin of pork, boned with skin removed
½ teaspoon red food colouring diluted with water
50 g (2 tablespoons) hoisin sauce
20 ml (1 tablespoon) mirin or dry sherry
20 ml (1 tablespoon) soy sauce
3 cloves garlic, chopped
2½ cm (1 inch) fresh green ginger, grated
3 star anise, crushed
20 ml (1 tablespoon) sesame oil
25 g (1 tablespoon) sugar
20 ml (1 tablespoon) fish sauce

Using rubber gloves, rub pork all over with red food colouring. Combine remaining ingredients in food processor bowl and blend well. Pour marinade over pork, covering well. Refrigerate overnight turning pork from time to time. Other cuts of pork can be used in this recipe.

To cook, preheat oven to very hot 230°C (450°F). Place marinated pork on a roasting rack and cook for 10 minutes. Baste with marinade and reduce oven heat to 180°C (350°F). Cook for 1 hour, basting now and again.

Remove from oven and allow to rest at least 15 minutes. Slice thinly and arrange on serving platter. It is delicious cold.

CUCUMBER BOATS

4 long green cucumbers
pickled garlic
marinated ginger
4 hard-boiled eggs
spring onions to serve

Remove cucumber skin, slice lengthwise and scoop out seeds with a small spoon. Serve filled with pickled garlic, marinated ginger, hard-boiled eggs, shelled, sliced and salted. Accompany with spring onions, cleaned and refreshed in soda water and ice cubes.

KHAO PHAD
FRIED RICE

1 cup of cooked rice per person
500 g (1 lb) cooked beef, pork, chicken or prawns,
   diced into small pieces
100 ml (5 tablespoons) vegetable oil
3 medium onions, diced
3 cloves garlic, thinly sliced
25 g (1 tablespoon) red curry paste
3 whole eggs, lightly beaten with a fork
40 ml (2 tablespoons) fish sauce
200 g (7 oz) snake beans, cut into 2.5 cm (1 inch)
   pieces, blanched and refreshed

Heat oil in a wok, add onions, garlic and stir-fry until garlic starts to colour. Add curry paste, stirring well. Toss in meat to blend. Make a hole in centre of mixture, add eggs and stir well. Add rice and mix well together. Add fish sauce, snake beans heating through. Serve on a platter.

NAM KATI SAI MED MANG LUCK
COCONUT MILK WITH SWEET BASIL SEEDS

40 g (1 ½ oz) sweet basil seeds
2 fresh young coconuts
800 ml (3¼ cups) coconut cream
200 g (6½ oz) brown or palm sugar

Sweet basil seeds can be found in Asian food stores. They are often used in sweets or to thicken soups and milk. They give an interesting texture similar to caviar eggs.

Place sweet basil seeds in a bowl and cover with cold water. Stir to loosen and soak for 30 minutes. Strain water from the seeds and divide between 8 bowls. To take on a picnic, use plastic containers.

Crack young coconuts with a heavy cleaver. Save the juice if you can for a delicious drink. Use a spoon to scrape out the soft flesh from the coconut shell and add to basil seeds. Warm coconut cream with sugar until dissolved. Allow to cool before adding to coconut meat and basil seeds. Chill well, or serve over ice cubes.

TROPICAL FRUITS OF THE SEASON

Serve fresh fruit, peeled and cut into manageable slices.

NAM MANAO
LIMEADE

See recipe in Kathin Lunch.

LUNCH IN SUKHOTAI

In 1237 the King of Cambodia sent a general to restore order among the Tai people in the north of his empire, of which Suk'Ot'Ai was the capital. The Cambodians were totally defeated and the Tai chiefs took over the town.

The ancient capital of Sukhotai was founded in 1238 when the Thais freed themselves from Cambodia, forming the Kingdom of Sukhotai Syam. Situated on the 'Friendship' highway going north, Sukhotai means the 'dawn of happiness'.

Today it is one of the archaeological wonders of the world. Ruins of huge temples and beautiful sculptures of Buddha are to be seen everywhere, each more impressive than the last. The road through the distant green rainforest-covered mountains leads to Chiangmai.

We had a simple lunch sitting under a fiery poinciana tree, surrounded by antiquity.

The salad was made from tiny freshwater shrimps combined with crisp green mango. As a second dish a plate of crisp fried, flaked, smoked fish followed. There was a platter of fresh vegetables quickly cooked in coconut milk and topped with pearly coconut cream.

The inventive cook prepared two delicious courses from a piece of belly pork. The skin had been removed and cooked crisp for use in the salad. Meat taken from the ribs was cubed to prepare the most delicious sweet candied pork I have ever tasted. The bones went into a pot to make stock for the soup. When served, the soup contained jade-green chunks of bitter gourd and tiny stuffed squid.

To finish our lunch, little cups were turned out to reveal sweet-smelling coconut puddings; refreshing and cool. We drank large glasses of iced tea, which was more to show that the water had been boiled. No one mentioned the ice cubes! It was hard to leave such a majestic setting of the past.

YAM GOONG
SHRIMP SALAD

PLA FOO
FRIED SMOKED FISH

PAK TOM KATI
VEGETABLES IN COCONUT MILK

MOO WAN
SWEET CANDIED PORK

GAENG CHUD PLA MUEK SAI MOO
SOUP WITH BITTER GOURD AND STUFFED SQUID

KAO HORM MALI
STEAMED FRAGRANT RICE

KHANOM TALAI
STEAMED COCONUT PUDDING

YAM GOONG
SHRIMP SALAD

1 kg (2 lbs) tiny shrimps or prawns
2–3 green mangoes
salt and pepper
8 cloves garlic, thinly sliced and fried crisp
6 shallots (red onions), sliced and fried crisp
100 g (4 oz) bacon, diced and crisp fried
3 limes, juice only
100 g (4 oz) peanuts, toasted and chopped
½ cup coriander leaves
shredded coconut, toasted, to garnish

Cook shrimps in salted water, drain and refresh in iced water. Peel, leaving tail intact. Peel mangoes and slice into thin strips.

Season shrimps with salt and pepper in a bowl. Toss in crisp fried garlic, shallots, bacon and lime juice and mix well together. Add mango strips and mix lightly together with peanuts and coriander. Serve garnished with shredded coconut.

PLA FOO
FRIED SMOKED FISH

Catfish (Pla Dook) is one of my favourite fresh water fish. It is usually sold live in the markets, and, therefore, has the extra texture only found in fresh fish. In Thailand, it is skewered whole, after gutting, and smoked over a low fire: it is a combination of grilling and smoking. At Sukhothai the fish was crisp fried and served with ice tea. It is terrific with cold beer. Use smoked trout, smoked cod or smoked haddock as a substitute to catfish.

500 g (1 lb) flaked smoked fish
oil for deep frying
6 shallots (red onions) thinly sliced
2 small red chillis, thinly sliced
50 ml (2 tablespoons) fish sauce
coriander leaves to garnish

Flake fish, removing all skin and bones. Heat oil and sprinkle flaked fish into frying basket. Lower into hot oil and fry until crisp. Remove and drain on paper towels. Toss crisp fish with shallots, chillis and fish sauce.

Turn on to a platter or banana leaf and garnish with coriander leaves.

PAK TOM KATI
VEGETABLES IN COCONUT MILK

500 ml (2 cups) coconut milk
15 g (½ tablespoon) salt
snake beans
wing beans
baby corn or candle corn
cauliflower
small zucchini
baby squash
40 ml (2 tablespoons) coconut cream
cracked black pepper

All vegetables should be fresh, washed and cut into bite-size pieces. The amount varies according to the number of people.

Bring coconut milk to boil with the salt. Add selected vegetables and bring back to boil. Simmer for 2 minutes. The vegetables should remain crisp. Remove and drain. Spoon over coconut cream and sprinkle with cracked black pepper.

MOO WAN
SWEET CANDIED PORK

1 ½ kg (3 lbs) belly pork, skin removed
2 tablespoons garlic, finely sliced
125 ml (½ cup) white vinegar
2 tablespoons chilli paste
125 g (4 oz) brown sugar or palm sugar
30 ml (1 ½ tablespoons) light soy sauce
30 ml (1 ½ tablespoons) fish sauce

Cut pork into bite-size pieces. Cook in a wok with garlic, adding a cup of water and the vinegar. Bring to boil and simmer, stirring to stop pork from sticking to the wok. Add a little more water if it evaporates. Continue cooking until pork is tender. By that time the water will have evaporated and the pork should be lightly coloured.

Add chilli paste, sugar, soy sauce and fish sauce. Stir vigorously until pork caramelises to a dark brown colour. Remove from wok with a slotted spoon leaving any fat behind.

In this delicious dish the vinegar cuts the strong smell of the pork and the finished result is sweet and hot.

GAENG CHUD PLA MUEK SAI MOO
SOUP WITH BITTER GOURD AND STUFFED SQUID

8 cleaned squid tubes
250 g (½ lb) minced pork
2 shallots (red onions), chopped
2 cloves garlic, chopped
10 peppercorns
1 teaspoon salt
1 whole egg
1–2 fresh bitter gourds
½ cup coriander leaves

Stock

approximately 8 pork rib bones
2 litres (8 cups) water
3 stalks celery

Sankaya Fak Thong: Coconut custard in a pumkin.

To make stock:

Place rib bones in a saucepan with 2 litres (8 cups) water and three stalks of celery. Bring to boil and simmer for ½ hour. Strain and reserve.

To make soup:

Pound shallots, garlic and peppercorns in a mortar and pestle to make a smooth paste. Add to minced pork, mixing in egg to make a farce. Stuff squid tubes half full. The squid shrinks and the stuffing expands.

Cut bitter gourd in half lengthways and then into 2.5 cm (1 inch) pieces. Blanch in boiling water to remove some of the bitterness.

Simmer squid and bitter gourd in strained stock for 10 minutes. Season with salt and pepper. Serve garnished with coriander leaves.

KAO HORM MALI
STEAMED FRAGRANT RICE

See recipe in glossary.

KHANOM TALAI
STEAMED COCONUT PUDDING

160 g (8 tablespoons) brown sugar or palm sugar
80 ml (4 tablespoons) hot water
250 ml (1 cup) coconut milk
140 g (7 tablespoons) rice flour
250 ml (1 cup) coconut cream

Dissolve sugar in hot water and add coconut milk. Sift 100 g (5 tablespoons) rice flour and mix to a smooth batter. Divide mixture between 8 small moulds filling each two-thirds full. Place in a bamboo steamer over boiling water and cook for 15 minutes.

Stir remaining sifted rice flour into coconut cream. Divide this amongst steamed moulds. Return to steamer for another 20 minutes.

Remove and allow to cool. Serve tepid or chilled turned out on to serving dish.

Miang Pla Too: Salad of sardines or mackerel.

DINNER AT NAKORN SAWAN

In the north of Thailand, on the banks of the Chao Phya River is Nakorn Sawan, which means 'heavenly village'. The city is on the right bank of the river, just at the point where the River Nan enters the main waterway. It is a prosperous town, important to the people of the north as a despatch point for goods transported by road and river.

During the monsoon season the river rushes by, wide and deep. I went there during the dry season, when the banks were high and steep. At that time local fish was in short supply, but there were other taste sensations in store for us.

For our meal we chose a Thai dish popular with the people of the north and Laos. It is a type of steak tartare, and they eat it raw with hot chilli sauce as a dip. The recipe for larp isan, spicy minced meat is more acceptable to our palate if the meat is quickly blanched. It improves the appearance of the salad, which is usually served with glutinous rice. The Thais form a ball of rice with their fingers and dip into the larp.

The golden crisp-fried stuffed eggs are surprisingly succulent. Using green papaya in the sweet and sour soup gives it a fresh and interesting texture; green beans, cabbage and even chunks of pineapple can be used as a substitute.

Chicken in coconut is one of the dishes I love to cook at home. A rich dish, cooked in coconut milk and coated with a reduced sauce, it is rewarding to prepare.

Sugar bananas in a sweet coconut sauce, and usually served as a snack, were spiked with black beans and made a 'heavenly' ending to our meal.

LARP ISAN
SPICY MINCED MEAT

KAI KWAM
FRIED STUFFED EGGS

GAENG TOM SOM
SWEET AND SOUR SOUP

GAI OB NAM KATI
CHICKEN IN COCONUT MILK

KAO HORM MALI
STEAMED FRAGRANT RICE

KLUAY BUAT
SUGAR BANANAS IN COCONUT CREAM

LARP ISAN
SPICY MINCED MEAT

40 g (2 tablespoons) long grained rice
1 litre (4 cups) water
500 g (1 lb) minced topside beef
100 ml (5 tablespoons) fresh lime juice
1 cup mint leaves
4 fresh red chillis, crushed, (prik e noo suan)
4 fresh green chillis, crushed (prik e noo kaset)
3 stalks lemon grass, tender part only, sliced finely
6 shallots (red onions), sliced finely
40 ml (2 tablespoons) fish sauce

Fry rice in a dry pan until it turns a pale gold. Pound in a mortar and pestle until crushed. Bring water to boil in a pot. Add beef stirring to separate.

As soon as beef has coloured, strain in a sieve and turn into a bowl. Pour over lime juice and mix in mint leaves with ground rice. Add crushed red and green chillis, with lemon grass and shallots. Sprinkle with fish sauce and toss well together. Turn on to a serving platter and garnish with mint leaves.

KAI KWAM
FRIED STUFFED EGGS

8 large hard-boiled eggs
125 g (4 oz) minced pork
125 g (4 oz) cooked prawn meat, chopped
125 g (4 oz) cooked crabmeat
40 ml (2 tablespoons) coconut cream
2 tablespoons coriander stalks and leaves, chopped
fresh ground pepper
20 ml (1 tablespoon) fish sauce
oil for deep frying

Batter

140 g (1 cup) flour
5 g (1 teaspoon) baking powder
5 g (1 teaspoon) salt

5 g (1 teaspoon) sugar
40 ml (2 tablespoons) vegetable oil
250 ml (1 cup) water

Peel hard-boiled eggs and cut in half. Place yolks in a bowl and reserve whites on a platter.

Mash yolks, add minced pork, prawns and crabmeat, mixing well together. Add coconut cream, coriander, pepper and fish sauce, stirring to a firm paste. Divide this mixture between the 16 egg whites. With your hands form the shape of a whole egg, and put to one side, Prepare batter mixture.

To make batter:

Quickly whisk batter ingredients together and use immediately.

Dip stuffed eggs into batter and deep fry until crisp, keeping the filling side downwards. Drain on paper towels and serve.

GAENG TOM SOM
SWEET AND SOUR SOUP

1 kg (2 lbs) pork, chicken or fish
3 shallots (red onions) chopped
1 teaspoon peppercorns
3 cloves garlic
25 g (1 tablespoon) shrimp paste
oil for frying
1½ litres (6 cups) water
2½ cm (1 inch) fresh green ginger, peeled and finely chopped
125 ml (½ cup) tamarind water (see glossary)
1 green paw paw, peeled and thinly sliced
sugar to taste
3 spring onions, cut into 2½ cm (1 inch) lengths to garnish

Pound shallots, peppercorns, garlic and shrimp paste or blend in a food processor. Fry paste in a little hot oil for 1 minute. Add water and bring to boil.

Cut selected meat into bite-size pieces, add to stock with ginger and tamarind water. Simmer until meat is nearly cooked. Add paw paw and bring back to boil. Check seasoning, add a little sugar, although the flavour should be slightly sour. Garnish with chopped spring onions and serve.

GAI OB NAM KATI
CHICKEN IN COCONUT MILK

1 no. 16–17 (3–4 lbs) fresh chicken
1 litre (4 cups) coconut milk
6 dried chillis, chopped
50 g (2 tablespoons) peanuts
10 peppercorns
2 stalks lemon grass, tender part only, chopped
5 shallots (red onions), chopped
3 cloves garlic, chopped
25 g (1 tablespoon) sugar
10 ml (1 teaspoon) shrimp paste
oil for frying
2 fresh red chillis, chopped, to garnish
2 makrut leaves, chopped, to garnish

Place chicken in casserole, cover with 3 cups coconut milk and bring to boil. Reduce heat to simmer and cook for 45 minutes, covered with lid. Remove chicken and keep warm.

Pound dried chillis, peanuts, peppercorns, lemon grass, shallots, garlic, sugar and shrimp paste or blend in a food processor. Heat a little oil in a pan and fry paste for 2 minutes. Add 1 cup of coconut milk to deglaze the pan and reduce quantity to one-third.

Return chicken to casserole, turning over and over until well-coated with sauce. Remove to a serving platter and spoon over remaining sauce. Garnish with chopped chillis and makrut leaves.

KAO HORM MALI
STEAMED FRAGRANT RICE

See recipe in glossary.

KLUAY BUAT
SUGAR BANANAS IN COCONUT CREAM

12–16 sugar bananas or 8 large bananas
250 ml (1 cup) coconut cream or thick coconut milk
50 g (2 tablespoons) brown sugar or palm sugar

Peel sugar bananas; if using larger ones, peel, cut in half and lengthwise to make four pieces.

Warm coconut milk and stir in sugar to dissolve. Add bananas, bring to boil and simmer for 3 minutes. Remove from heat and allow to cool. Serve at room temperature, although the dish is still delicious when chilled.

FLAVOURED BANANA SAUCE

Sugar bananas are my favourite and I would like to add a sauce recipe. This sauce is delicious served with corn pancakes and over ice-cream.

5 ripe sugar bananas or 3 large bananas
juice of 1 lime or ½ lemon
1 tablespoon honey
250 ml (1 cup) cream
flavour with ½ teaspoon cinnamon powder
or
1 tablespoon minced crystallised ginger
or
25 ml (1 oz) dark rum

Peel bananas and chop coarsely. Place in blender or food processor, add lime juice, honey, cream and blend until smooth. Add your choice of flavouring or leave the natural taste. Serve as quickly as possible, before discolouration.

LUNCH AT WAT CHALERM

The 200 year-old temple of Wat Chalerm, located across the river from Nontha Buri boat landing is a place of extraordinary beauty. A lotus flower motif is repeated on the huge doors and shutters of the temple. Porcelain tiles on the walls have the same design. Although the temple is neglected, Buddhist monks still live in cottages around the ruins, adding to the peaceful atmosphere.

The temple dates from the reign of Rama III and is surrounded by two fortress-like walls. One wall has square towers with circular openings in the Chinese style of architecture.

At the front of the temple there is a large boat landing where the King used to farewell the Thai navy when they went to sea, before the founding of Bangkok in 1782.

Overlooking the river, the Nontha Buri landing is used by several restaurants as the perfect spot for al fresco dining, and we took advantage of the setting.

Our meal began with a salad of raw fish marinated in lime juice and fish sauce. We drank Thai beer with foam running down the sides of the glasses.

Crisp pork crackling was served neatly arranged in bite-size pieces; an unforgettable dish. Son-in-law eggs are always a popular standby, and were probably invented by a mother-in-law who found herself with another mouth to feed.   Sweet basil seeds were an unusual addition to the stuffed squid soup. They swell and thicken the soup and look like a garnish of caviar.

Crisp golden rings coloured with saffron are usually served with a sugar syrup. I prefer the delicate flavour of maple syrup.

YAM PLA
MARINATED FISH

MOO GROB
CRISP PORK CRACKLING

YAM THAENG KWA
SPICY CUCUMBER SALAD

KAI LOOK KOEI
SON-IN-LAW EGGS

TOM YAM PLA MUEK
SQUID SOUP WITH BASIL SEEDS

KAO HORM MALI
STEAMED FRAGRANT RICE

KHANOM TORD
GOLDEN RINGS

YAM PLA
MARINATED FISH

750 g (1½ lbs) coral trout or other white fish fillets
125 ml (½ cup) fresh lime juice
500 ml (2 cups) coconut milk
100 g (½ cup) fresh green peppercorns
3 stalks lemon grass, tender part only
60 ml (3 tablespoons) fish sauce
1 cup fresh mint leaves

Slice fish finely, place in a glass bowl and cover with lime juice. Put to one side while preparing other ingredients.

Lightly crush peppercorns in a mortar and pestle to bring out flavour. Cut lemon grass thinly across the stems. Add all ingredients to bowl with fish and mix well. Refrigerate at least 4 hours or overnight.

MOO GROB
CRISP PORK CRACKLING

1.5 kg (3 lbs) streaky belly pork with skin
1 teaspoon salt
1 tablespoon peppercorns
10 cloves garlic, crushed
3 whole coriander plants, root, stalk and leaves
oil for deep frying

Sauce

2 tablespoons chilli paste
40 ml (2 tablespoons) lime juice
25 g (1 tablespoon) sugar

Cover pork with water adding all above ingredients. Bring to boil, skim well, reduce to simmer until pork is cooked. Remove from stock and allow to cool. With a sharp knife or cleaver score pork skin at 2.5 cm (1 inch) intervals. Turn pork around and score at 1 cm (¼ inch) intervals. I use white vinegar to remove the strong smell of pork, rinsing two or three times. Dry pork in the sun or in the oven on a rack at 180°C (400°F) for 30 minutes.

When cool enough to handle, cut pork into slices across the grain. Heat oil and deep fry slices until the skin has crackled. Remove and drain on paper towels.

To make sauce:

Mix sauce ingredients well together until dissolved.

Cut pork slices into bite-size pieces and serve with sauce and spicy cucumber salad.

YAM THAENG KWA
SPICY CUCUMBER SALAD

See recipe 'Lunch with Michel Roux'.

KAI LOOK KOEI
SON-IN-LAW EGGS

8 hard-boiled eggs, peeled
vegetable oil for deep frying
80 g (4 tablespoons) brown sugar or palm sugar
40 ml (2 tablespoons) fish sauce
80 ml (4 tablespoons) tamarind water
6 shallots (red onions), thinly sliced, fried crisp
6 fresh red chillis thinly sliced, fried crisp
8 coriander leaves to garnish

Heat oil and fry hard-boiled eggs until crisp, golden and blistered. Remove and drain on paper towels.

In a wok, heat 2 tablespoons of oil and add sugar, fish sauce and tamarind water stirring to form a syrupy sauce. Pour over fried eggs, sprinkle with crisp shallots and chillis. Garnish with coriander leaves.

TOM YAM PLA MUEK
SQUID SOUP WITH BASIL SEEDS

1 kg (2 lbs) baby squid
300 g (10 oz) minced pork
½ teaspoon salt
1 clove garlic, crushed
½ teaspoon fresh ginger, grated
2 litres (8 cups) clear fish stock
4–8 fresh chillis to taste
4 stalks lemon grass, crushed and cut into
    5 cm (2 inch) lengths
6 teaspoons basil seeds
2 limes, juice only
1 cup coriander leaves to garnish

Clean baby squid and rinse in cold water. Mix the pork with salt, garlic and ginger. Half-fill squid tubes with farce; it will swell when cooking. Bring fish stock to boil with chillis and lemon grass and allow to simmer for 5 minutes. Add stuffed squid and basil seeds to stock and simmer for 3 minutes. Check seasoning. Flavour with lime juice and garnish with coriander leaves before serving.

KAO HORM MALI
STEAMED FRAGRANT RICE

See recipe in glossary.

KHANOM TORD
GOLDEN RINGS

1 teaspoon saffron powder
20 ml (1 tablespoon) hot water
200 g (1½ cups) plain flour
5 g (1 teaspoon) baking powder
5 g (1 teaspoon) salt
170 ml (⅔ cup) water
250 ml (1 cup) vegetable oil
250 ml (1 cup) maple syrup

Dissolve saffron in hot water. Sift flour and baking powder into bowl. Add saffron water, salt and remaining ⅔ cup of water, mixing to a smooth batter.

Heat oil in a shallow pan to a depth of 1 cm (½ inch). Make a cornet of greaseproof paper or use a piping bag with a fine nozzle. Pipe batter into hot oil in a circular motion. Fry until golden. Remove and drain on paper towels. Serve coated with maple syrup.

To make traditional Thai syrup, boil two cups of sugar with one cup of water for 10 minutes. Coat golden rings as above.

LUNCH AT SANAM LUANG

Lak Muang is the foundation stone, at the centre of Bangkok, from which all distances are measured. A huge oval space stretching from the Temple of the Emerald Buddha to Klong Lord, Sanam Luang, 'the royal plaza' is planted with old tamarind trees and at weekends it is transformed into a gigantic open-air market; an exciting experience for visitors.

The shopping area, occupied by canvas-covered stalls, is well organised selling everything from food, flowers, plants, orchids, textiles, clothes and books, to jewellery, antiques and animals. I shopped at the market to brighten the menu at the *Two Vikings*. I found legs of wild boar, deer, quail, grouse and wild duck in season. When I bought one hundred wild duck and paid for them the vendor said: 'Where is your car?' He was ready to load the quacking birds into the back!

I said: 'Excuse me, but they're still alive!'

He shrugged. 'Oh, but I can't do anything about that. I'm a Buddhist . . .

'And so am I, so what will we do?'

'If you pay another baht for each duck, I can find a Pakistani butcher who will do it.'

I told him that was a deal and left the stall, returning in an hour after spending a fortune on antiques. The ducks were ready in a couple of sacks, the two Buddhists were saved and the butcher was 100 baht better off.

Food stalls around the market are popular and business is brisk. I often sat down with my staff for lunch to have one of my favourite dishes: green duck curry with a side dish of crisp fried noodles. We would often fall for a huge bowl of spicy clams. We would order fried shrimp balls and a steaming pot of chicken soup flavoured with galangal and coconut milk. To finish there were lychees and sweet custard apples washed down with fresh crushed sugar-cane juice.

HOI LAI PAD PRIK
SPICY CLAMS

TORD MAN GOONG
FRIED SHRIMP BALLS

GAENG KEO WAN PET
GREEN DUCK CURRY

MEE KROB
CRISP FRIED NOODLES

DOM KA GAI
CHICKEN COCONUT SOUP

KAO HORM MALI
STEAMED FRAGRANT RICE

LEENCHEE GAB NOI NA
FRESH LYCHEES AND CUSTARD APPLES

HOI LAI PAD PRIK
SPICY CLAMS

Among the many delicious seafoods at the weekend market, are the small, shiny, smooth, sand- and sea-coloured clams, piled high in mountains. They are similar to Australian pippis.

1 kg (2 lbs) clams or pippis
125 ml (½ cup) cooking oil
2 cloves garlic, chopped
2.5 cm (1 inch) fresh ginger, finely chopped
4 red chillis, chopped
40 ml (2 tablespoons) fish sauce
25 g (1 tablespoon) chilli paste
125 ml (½ cup) dry white wine
salt to taste
chopped coriander leaves for garnish

Wash clams or pippis in several lots of cold water to remove sand. They are collected on the beach at low tide, and because they live in the sand they can be quite gritty.

Heat oil in wok and add garlic, ginger and chillis. Stir-fry for 2 minutes. Add clams, fish sauce, chilli paste and white wine. Toss well and cover to cook for 4 minutes, or until clams open. Remove to a serving platter, discarding any shells that have not opened.

Reduce stock by half. Season with salt to taste. Often clams may be salty enough. Pour stock over clams and garnish with coriander or parsley or dill.

TORD MAN GOONG
FRIED SHRIMP BALLS

500 g (1 lb) prawn meat
2 cloves garlic, chopped
2 egg whites
fresh ground pepper
20 ml (1 tablespoon) fish sauce
oil for frying

Pla Khow Lard Prik: Fried Red Emperor with white chilli sauce.

Place prawn meat, garlic, egg whites and fresh crushed pepper in the food processor bowl. Blend into a paste adding fish sauce. Remove to a bowl.

Heat a little oil in a frying pan. Form small round balls 3 cm (1 inch) and slightly flatten them. Fry in oil until golden brown, turning once. This should take about 2 minutes on each side. Remove and drain on paper towels. Serve with spicy cucumber salad (see Lunch with Michel Roux).

GAENG KEO WAN PET GREEN DUCK CURRY

250 ml (1 cup) coconut cream
75 g (3 tablespoons) green curry paste
1 no. 18 (3½ lbs) roasting duck
1 litre (4 cups) coconut milk
8 makrut leaves
6 fresh green chillis
20 sweet basil leaves
20 ml (1 tablespoon) fish sauce

Place coconut cream in a wok with green curry paste and stir to dissolve. Cook until cream has reduced by one-third. Cut duck into bite-size pieces and add to wok with curry coconut cream. Cook slowly turning duck pieces for 15 minutes. Add coconut milk and makrut leaves.

Continue to simmer slowly, stirring from time to time, for another 40 minutes or until duck is tender. Add chillis and basil leaves, stir and cook for another 5 minutes. Add fish sauce to season. Serve on a platter as part of a meal.

Above: Ho Mok Hoy Man Poo: *Steamed stuffed mussels.*
Below: Look Moo Don: *Steamed pearly meat balls.*

MEE KROB
CRISP FRIED NOODLES

½ packet rice sticks (rice vermicelli)
oil for deep frying

Sauce

oil for frying
10 cloves garlic, chopped
6 shallots (red onions), chopped
100 g (3 oz) minced pork
100 g (3 oz) minced chicken
100 g (3 oz) chopped prawns
300 g (10 oz) bean curd, chopped
6 eggs
120 g (½ cup) sugar
60 ml (3 tablespoons) vinegar
40 ml (2 tablespoons) fish sauce
pickled garlic to garnish
4 fresh red chillis, cut into strips, to garnish
100 g (4 oz) bean sprouts, to garnish
½ cup coriander leaves, to garnish

Deep-fry vermicelli in hot oil, turning over. It only takes seconds for them to turn golden brown. Remove from oil, drain on paper towels. Keep warm in a low oven to ensure they stay crisp.

To make sauce:

Heat a little oil in a wok and fry garlic and shallots to colour, add pork, chicken, prawn meat and stir-fry. Add bean curd and stir. Add eggs beaten with a fork and stir, turning mixture over and over. Stir until liquid has evaporated and only oil is left in the base of the wok. Add sugar and vinegar, stir-frying until absorbed.

When ready to serve toss noodles into sauce in the wok, turning gently over low heat. Season with fish sauce.

Turn on to a large platter, garnish with pickled garlic, red chilli strips, bean sprouts and coriander leaves.

DOM KA GAI
CHICKEN COCONUT SOUP

1 ½ litres (6 cups) water
6 pieces galangal, dried
2 stalks lemon grass, tender part only, crushed
2 fresh red chillis
500 g (1 lb) chicken meat
500 ml (2 cups) coconut milk
2 limes, juice only
20 ml (1 tablespoon) fish sauce
20 ml (1 tablespoon) chilli paste
basil leaves to garnish

Bring the water to boil with galangal, lemon grass and two chillis cut into
strips. Simmer for 10 minutes to release flavours. Remove skin from chicken
and cut meat into strips. Add to stock with coconut milk and return to boil.
Simmer adding lime or lemon juice, fish sauce and chilli paste. Serve
garnished with basil leaves.

KAO HORM MALI
STEAMED FRAGRANT RICE

See recipe in glossary.

LEENCHEE GAB NOI NA
FRESH LYCHEES AND CUSTARD APPLES

24 fresh lychees
4 custard apples

Peel lychees and place on crushed ice in a bowl. Cut custard apples in half
and surround the lychees on ice. Serve with dessert spoons and finger bowls.

DINNER AT KO SAMUI

The island Ko Samui, 'like a lump of jade in the blue sea', was my favourite place to get away from it all. Between late January and April, when the sea was calm, I would travel by boat and spend three days relaxing and painting on this peaceful island.

I stayed in a guest house near the most beautiful beach; a stretch of white sand lined with coconut palms leaning over the water.

Crystal-clear streams ran into the sea from the cool mountain waterfalls. On the island there were three million coconut palms and a coconut fibre factory. The coconuts grew so high in the trees that no man could reach them. Monkeys were trained to climb the trees, shaking the coconuts to select the ripe ones, twisting them free to fall on the ground.

As a secondary crop, pepper vines grew up most of the palm trunks, sprouting bunches of fresh green peppercorns. Leafy green durian trees (the most sublime of fruit) grew in clusters around the house.

We were served delicious dinners at the guest house, sitting on the verandah overlooking the beach.

While we sipped chilled whiskey and soda the cook prepared succulent chicken and pork satay. On the table there were platters with squid salad, an omelette stuffed with pork and vegetables and a spicy, dry chicken curry.

Bowls of steaming rice were served with dishes of fish sauce containing crushed green peppercorns replacing the usual chilli.

When the coconut cream custard and sticky rice were brought to the table, the moon was shining over the nearby islands. In the distance the islands looked like submerged mountain tops and sparkled like silver.

We finished our dinner as the waves rolled on to the beach in cascades of phosphorous light.

SATAY GAI
CHICKEN SATAY

NAM SATAY
PEANUT GARLIC SAUCE FOR SATAY

YAM PLA MUEK
SQUID SALAD

KAI YAK SAI
STUFFED OMELETTE

PANANG GAI
DRY CHICKEN CURRY

KAO HORM MALI
STEAMED FRAGRANT RICE

SANKAYA SAI KAO NIEO
COCONUT CREAM CUSTARD WITH STICKY RICE

SATAY GAI
CHICKEN SATAY

4 chicken breasts, meat only
   (or 500 g (1 lb) pork loin or fillet)
bamboo skewers

Marinade for satay

1 teaspoon curry paste
2 cloves garlic, chopped
½ teaspoon tumeric
20 ml (1 tablespoon) soy sauce
1 stalk lemon grass, tender part only, chopped
125 ml (½ cup) coconut milk

Slice chicken breasts into long thin slices. There should be 5 to 6 slices from each breast. Place in a bowl.

To make marinade:

Blend marinade ingredients in food processor to a smooth mixture. Pour marinade over chicken strips. Mix gently and allow to marinate for 2 hours. Thread on bamboo skewers and cook over charcoal or under broiler, turning once. Serve with garlic and peanut sauce (see next recipe) and spicy cucumber salad (see Lunch with Michel Roux).

NAM SATAY
PEANUT GARLIC SAUCE FOR SATAY

2 cups raw shelled peanuts
oil for frying
20 cloves garlic, chopped
10–15 fresh red chillis, chopped
150 g (5 oz) brown sugar or raw sugar
100 ml (5 tablespoons) tamarind water
500 ml (2 cups) coconut milk
salt

Place peanuts in a roasting pan and cook in oven at 185°C (350°F) to loosen skins. Remove from oven and rub peanuts in a kitchen towel to remove skins. Crush peanuts in food processor.

In a wok, fry garlic in a little oil for a few seconds, adding chillis, crushed peanuts and sugar. Stir in tamarind water and coconut milk, mixing well. Season with salt. Keep stirring while cooking the paste; it will take a while and is ready when the oil separates from the mixture. Remove from heat and cool.

The sauce will keep for months refrigerated in a glass jar. Use as required with satay.

YAM PLA MUEK
SQUID SALAD

500 g (1 lb) squid tubes, cleaned
1 tablespoon chilli sauce or chilli paste
½ cup fresh lime juice or lemon juice
2 stalks lemon grass, tender part only, sliced thinly
6 shallots (red onions) or 10 spring onions, sliced thinly
20 ml (1 tablespoon) fish sauce
1 cup fresh mint leaves to garnish

Slice cleaned squid tubes into 3 mm (⅛ inch) rings. Rinse in cold water and drain in a colander. Dissolve chilli paste in lime or lemon juice, adding lemon grass, sliced shallots and fish sauce. Wash mint leaves and remove from stalks.

Bring a pot of water to boil. Throw in squid slices, bring back to boil, stir, strain and rinse under cold running water. Drain and while still warm add to dressing mixture, tossing well. Garnish with mint leaves and serve at room temperature. This salad can be prepared in advance.

KAI YAK SAI
STUFFED OMELETTE

4 cloves garlic, chopped
12 green peppercorns
4 coriander roots and stalks, chopped, retain
   leaves for garnish
60 ml (3 tablespoons) vegetable oil
155 g (5 oz) minced pork or chicken
4 shallots (red onions), chopped
1 tomato, diced
6–8 snake beans, cut into 5 mm (¼ inch) pieces
20 ml (1 tablespoon) fish sauce
8 whole eggs

To make stuffing:

Pound garlic, peppercorns, coriander stalks and roots or blend well
together in a food processor. Heat half the vegetable oil in a wok and fry
paste for 1 minute. Add pork or chicken and stir-fry until it changes colour.
Add shallots, tomato and snake beans, seasoning with fish sauce. Mix
together well and set aside to keep warm.

To make omelettes:

Wipe the wok clean with a paper towel and heat half of remaining oil. Beat
eggs with a fork and pour half the mixture into wok, shaking to spread
mixture evenly. Spoon half the stuffing in a line across the centre of the
eggs. Fold in half and slide on to a plate.

   Heat oil and repeat cooking process with remaining eggs and filling
mixture. Garnish omelettes with coriander leaves and serve.

PANANG GAI
DRY CHICKEN CURRY

750 g (1½ lbs) chicken meat
1 teaspoon fresh or tinned green peppercorns, crushed
50 g (½ cup) plain flour
100 ml (5 tablespoons) vegetable oil
50 g (2 tablespoons) red curry paste
250 ml (1 cup) coconut cream

25 g (1 tablespoon) sugar
40 ml (2 tablespoons) fish sauce
60 g (½ cup) roasted peanuts, chopped
basil leaves to garnish

Remove skin from chicken and cut into bite-size pieces. Rub crushed peppercorns into meat and toss in flour. Heat oil in a wok and stir-fry chicken pieces until well coloured and nearly cooked. Remove chicken to a platter and set aside. Pour most of the oil from the wok, add curry paste and stir-fry for 2 minutes. Stir in coconut cream, sugar, fish sauce and peanuts stirring well for 5 minutes. Toss in chicken and coat with thick sauce. Turn out on a serving platter and garnish with basil leaves.

KAO HORM MALI
STEAMED FRAGRANT RICE

See recipe in glossary.

SANKAYA SAI KAO NIEO
COCONUT CREAM CUSTARD WITH STICKY RICE

2 cups cooked sticky rice (see Mangoes with
   Sticky Rice in Lunch with Michel Roux)
2 large eggs
125 g (4 oz) brown sugar or palm sugar
250 ml (1 cup) coconut cream

Line the base of soufflé dishes or moulds with a thick layer of cooked sticky rice. (Use leftover from Mango with Sticky Rice.) Place in a bamboo steamer over boiling water to heat the rice.

Mix together eggs, sugar and coconut cream in a saucepan and heat through gently, dissolving sugar. Pour egg custard over rice in moulds and steam slowly until custard is set. Remove from steamer to cool.

Serve topped with coconut cream and toasted shredded coconut or ice-cream.

BREAKFAST ON THE RIVER KWAI

In my early days in Thailand I used to board a raft in the north and ride along the length of the river. This was before the building of dams for hydro-electricity and progress. The scenery was spectacular: soaring mountain gorges, dense tropical rainforest, innumerable waterfalls, some high and majestic, others gently cascading over smooth rocks.

The river winds its way through many provinces connecting towns and villages by numerous canals. Life on the river was fascinating. Produce from the northern region moved on barges to Bangkok — huge teak logs chained together and looking like floating islands topped with a little hut for the caretaker, often travelling with his family. Rafts sometimes moved in a group although each was independent. River adventurers could sleep in one thatched hut, with another for the men who handled the raft and did the cooking.

Our morning meal was the most memorable, mainly because passengers were asleep by 9 p.m. and up at sunrise. We would wake to smoking charcoal which would soon turn into glowing embers as breakfast was prepared. Each morning we collected fresh fruit from riverside landings or vendors would paddle up to the raft with supplies.

Some mornings we would just have watery boiled rice with small dried fish quickly roasted over the fire. Salted eggs, broken on to a plate were cooked over a steamer. Depending on supplies, the rice soup could be rich and delicious.

Sometimes we had Gai Swan, made with the skin of the chicken we ate the night before.

One morning we were served the most delicious pancakes made from fresh corn and small river shrimps. Cooked in a cast-iron pan over a charcoal fire, they were served hot and crisp at our breakfast table. I remember with delight the texture and subtle flavour of these pancakes.

Mock jackfruit seeds are sweet and filling, a delightful snack at any time. After a cup of pungent black coffee or strong Thai tea we knew we could face the day's adventures on the mighty river, drifting south to Bangkok.

KAO TOM GOONG-PLA
RICE SOUP WITH PRAWNS AND FISH

KAI KEM
PRESERVED SALTED EGGS

GAI SWAN
HEAVENLY CHICKEN

TORD MAN KAOPOT
FRIED CORN CAKES

MED KANOON
MOCK JACKFRUIT SEEDS

KAO TOM GOONG-PLA
RICE SOUP WITH PRAWNS AND FISH

3 cups of steamed rice from the day before
1.5 litres (6 cups) water or fish stock
8 large prawns (shrimp)
500 g (1 lb) fish fillets
2.5 cm (1 inch) fresh ginger root, peeled
1 celery stalk
2 fresh red chillis
4 shallots (red onions) or spring onions
8 cloves garlic
40 ml (2 tablespoons) fish sauce
40 ml (2 tablespoons) vegetable oil
coriander leaves to garnish

Place rice in a saucepan, add water or stock and bring to boil. Simmer for 1 minute and remove from heat.

Shell and devein prawns. Cut fish into 16 pieces. Cut ginger into fine strips, slice celery stalk and cut chillis into strips. Peel and slice shallots finely. Peel and finely slice garlic, fry in oil until golden.

Bring rice back to boil, add prawns, fish, celery, ginger, chillis, onions and season with fish sauce. Allow to simmer for 3 minutes. Sprinkle with fried garlic and oil. Garnish with coriander leaves. Serve hot.

This soup can be served with a raw egg in each bowl, topped with boiling soup.

KAI KEM
PRESERVED SALTED EGGS

See recipe in glossary.

GAI SWAN
HEAVENLY CHICKEN

chicken skin, removed when preparing other dishes
200 g (6 oz) prawn meat
200 g (6 oz) white fish fillets
½ tablespoon fresh ginger, peeled and grated
10 ml (½ tablespoon) fish sauce
banana leaves .
vegetable oil

Sauce

500 ml (2 cups) chicken stock
40 ml (2 tablespoons) soy sauce
½ teaspoon shrimp paste
2 tablespoons marinated ginger, finely chopped
40 g (2 tablespoons) cornflour, dissolved in
    some cold chicken stock
fresh red chillis, cut in strips, to garnish
coriander leaves to garnish

Mix prawns and fish in food processor with grated ginger and fish sauce to
form a smooth paste. Lay chicken skins on a flat surface and remove any
excess fat. Spread paste evenly over skin, about 5 mm (¼ inch) thick. Place
on banana leaves, skin side up and brush with vegetable oil. Cook in a
bamboo basket over gently boiling water for 10 to 15 minutes.

To make sauce:

Heat chicken stock, soy sauce, shrimp paste and marinated ginger together
and simmer for 3 minutes. Thicken with cornflour mixed into cold chicken
stock, stirring well.

Remove steamed chicken skins from banana leaves and cut into bite-size
pieces. Coat with sauce and garnish with chilli strips and coriander leaves.

TORD MAN KAOPOT
CORN PANCAKES

750 ml (3 cups) fresh corn kernels
2 large eggs, beaten
2 tablespoons cornflour
500 g (1 lb) tiny shrimps, shelled
2 tablespoons coriander stalk, chopped
2 cloves garlic, chopped
10 peppercorns, fresh green or dried, crushed
1 tablespoon raw sugar
40 ml (2 tablespoons) fish sauce
oil for frying

Combine corn kernels with eggs and cornflour in a bowl and stir in shrimp.
Pound coriander stalks, garlic and peppercorns. Add paste to corn mixture
and season with sugar and fish sauce. Mix well together and allow to stand
for 15 minutes.

Heat a heavy cast-iron pan and brush with oil. When the pan is hot, add 1
tablespoon of pancake mixture. Cook on both sides until brown and crisp.
They should be about 7–8 cm (3 inches) in diameter. The mixture will cook
quickly and is most delicious.

MED KANOON
MOCK JACKFRUIT SEEDS

225 g (½ lb) dry white lentils
125 g (4 oz) grated coconut
500 g (1 lb) sugar
350 ml (1 ½ cups) water
5 egg yolks
jasmine essence

Soak lentils overnight in cold water. Cook in a bamboo steamer until soft and mash with a fork while still warm. Leave to cool.

Combine with grated coconut and 150 g (5 oz) of the sugar, blend well. Shape mixture into the size of a grape or the seeds of a jackfruit. Bring water to boil with a drop of jasmine essence, add remaining sugar, stir until dissolved and reduce to simmer.

Place egg yolks in a bowl and beat with a fork. Dip 'lentil grapes' into egg yolk to coat well, then drop them into the simmering syrup. Cook for 5 minutes, remove and drain on a wire rack. Cool and chill before serving.

SONGKRAN DINNER

In the dry season when the earth is scorched by the heat of the sun and the nights are hot and steaming we celebrate the beginning of the Buddhist year. Songkran falls between the 13th and 15th April, and is a festival with floats, dancers and bands constantly moving through the streets. Anyone who wishes you well or just feels like it, can throw water over you and they expect you to return the compliment. You must dress for the day and wear clothes you don't care about. There is a jovial atmosphere with lots of laughter.

I spent Songkran in Chiangmai, the northern capital and celebrated the water festival of Mother Earth. The city is full of splendid old wooden houses surrounded by lush gardens. The temples, rich with wood carving, are left as an art form, a reminder of the city's golden past.

We had dinner in an old house opposite Wat Chet Yod, 'the temple of the seven spires', which dates back to 1455 and is an exquisite example of northern temple architecture. King Tilokraj built the temple in the year 2000 on the Buddhist calendar as a symbol of commemoration.

The dinner began with steamed sago filled with spicy chicken and crispy golden prawn balls. We were served 'galloping horses', a delightful combination of pork, prawns and peanuts heaped on fresh pineapple pieces.

Piquant spareribs were barbecued in the garden and came to the table with a resplendent whole fish, crisp fried and topped with a sweet and sour ginger sauce.

Platters and bowls were made from intricately hand-hammered silver; a special of Chiangmai.

The festival dinner finished with foi thong; fine skeins of 'golden silk' laid on a cinnamon leaf in a tiny silver bowl with a jasmine flower on the side, just enough for one mouthful.

Above: Moo Wan: Sweet candied pork.
Below: Gaeng Chud Pla Muek Sai Moo: Soup with bitter gourd and stuffed squid.

SAKU SAI GAI
CHICKEN AND SAGO BALLS

TORD MAN GOONG
GOLDEN PRAWN BALLS

MA HO
GALLOPING HORSES

SRI KRUNG MOO
PORK SPARE RIBS

PLA BRIO-WAN
FRIED SNAPPER IN GINGER SAUCE

KAO HORM MALI
STEAMED FRAGRANT RICE

FOI THONG
GOLDEN SILK

Above: Nam Manao: Limeade.
Below right: Kao Pad: Fried rice. Below middle: Carved chilled raw vegetables. Below left: Nam Prik: Hot chilli sauce.

SAKU SAI GAI
CHICKEN AND SAGO BALLS

500 g (1 lb) small sago
500 ml (2 cups) hot water
600 g (20 oz) chicken meat, minced
2 coriander roots, chopped
10 green peppercorns, fresh or tinned
3 cloves garlic, chopped
3 shallots (red onions), chopped
40 ml (2 tablespoons) vegetable oil
20 ml (1 tablespoon) fish sauce
25 g (1 tablespoon) sugar
lettuce leaves to serve
chilli strips to garnish
coriander leaves to garnish

Place sago in a bowl and cover with hot water, and stir to separate the pearls. The sago will absorb the water and swell.

Pound coriander roots, peppercorns, garlic and shallots to a smooth paste. Fry paste for 2 minutes in oil, add fish sauce, sugar, minced chicken and mix well together.

To assemble, mould a small amount of sago into flattened balls. Place a little chicken farce in the centre and smooth sago around it. Continue to shape balls until all farce has been used.

Place balls in a bamboo steamer over boiling water and cook until sago is clear and shiny. The chicken will also be cooked.

Serve in small lettuce leaves garnished with coriander and chilli strips. Pork or fish can be substituted for the chicken.

TORD MAN GOONG
GOLDEN PRAWN BALLS

1 kg (2 lbs) prawn meat
125 g (5 oz) pork fat (speck)
3 slices white bread, crusts removed
20 water chestnuts, finely chopped
1 teaspoon fresh green ginger, grated
3 egg yolks
1 egg white
vegetable oil for frying

Salt and Szechuan Pepper mixture

2 tablespoons Szechuan pepper (wild peppers)
3 tablespoons salt

Place prawn meat and pork fat in food processor and blend to a smooth paste. Soak bread in a little stock or water. Squeeze excess moisture from bread and place in a bowl with prawn-pork farce. Add water chestnuts, ginger and egg yolks, mixing well. Season with salt. Beat egg white and fold into farce.

With a small spoon shape walnut-size balls, dipping your hands into cold water. Shallow fry in vegetable oil for 2 to 3 minutes, turning over, until golden brown. Drain on paper towels. Serve with Salt and Szechuan Pepper mixture.

To make salt and pepper mixture:

Place both salt and pepper in a dry pan and roast over low heat. Shake pan constantly until mixture starts to smoke. Pound finely in a mortar and pestle. Use with fried or roasted meat.

MA HO
GALLOPING HORSES

1 large pineapple
4 cloves garlic, peeled and chopped
2 tablespoons coriander root and stalk, chopped
20 green peppercorns, fresh or canned
80 ml (4 tablespoons) peanut or vegetable oil
4 shallots (red onions), chopped
300 g (10 oz) minced, lean pork
150 g (5 oz) prawn meat, chopped
120 g (4 oz) roasted peanuts, crushed finely
30 g (1 oz) raw sugar
40 ml (2 tablespoons) fish sauce
2–3 red chillis, cut into fine strips for garnish
coriander leaves for garnish

Peel and core the pineapple. Cut into 1 cm (½ inch) slices and then into
bite-size chunks. Place on a serving platter.

Mix together garlic, coriander root and stalk, peppercorns and peanut oil in
food processor until smooth. Pour mixture into a frying pan and cook over
a medium heat for 20 seconds, stirring well.

Add minced pork, prawns and stir-fry. Add crushed peanuts, sugar and
fish sauce, stirring well. Remove and allow to cool.

Place a tablespoon of cooked mixture on each piece of pineapple.
Garnish with red chilli strips and coriander leaves. Serve at room
temperature or chill until required.

SRI KRUNG MOO
PORK SPARE RIBS

1 ½ kg (3 lbs) pork spare ribs, cut from belly pork,
   with skin removed

Marinade

6 cloves garlic, chopped
2.5 cm (1 inch) fresh green ginger, peeled and grated
1 cup pineapple, crushed
10 fresh red chillis, finely chopped
250 ml (1 cup) vinegar
80 ml (⅓ cup) oil
125 ml (½ cup) tomato paste
40 ml (2 tablespoons) soy sauce
2 teaspoons salt

Place spare ribs in a glass bowl. Combine marinade ingredients well and
pour over spare ribs. Rub marinade well into meat to cover. Refrigerate all
day or overnight.

   To cook, heat oven to 200°C (350°F). Place spare ribs on rack in roasting
pan, spreading evenly. Cook for 40 minutes basting often with marinade.
Serve on platter as part of meal.

   Spare ribs can also be barbecued on hotplate over glowing coals.

PLA BRIO-WAN
FRIED SNAPPER IN GINGER SAUCE

1 2 kg (4 lbs) whole snapper or red emperor, cleaned
   and scaled, with head intact
1 litre (4 cups) oil for frying
salt and pepper

Sauce

60 ml (3 tablespoons) vinegar
100 g (4 tablespoons) brown sugar or palm sugar
125 ml (½ cup) water
40 ml (2 tablespoons) soy sauce
8 shallots (red onions), chopped
10 cm (4 inches) fresh green ginger, peeled and
   finely chopped
2 limes, juice only
20 g (1 tablespoon) cornflour mixed with 80 ml
   (4 tablespoons) water
chilli strips to garnish
coriander leaves to garnish

To cook sauce:

Place vinegar, sugar, water, soy sauce in saucepan and bring to boil. Add shallots and ginger, cooking for 5 minutes. Add lime juice. Add cornflour mixture a little at a time, stirring well. The sauce should not be too thick. Keep warm.

To cook fish:

Heat oil in large wok. Season fish with salt and pepper. Carefully lower fish into hot oil and fry until crisp and golden. Turn over carefully and cook on other side. Remove and drain on paper towels.

   Place fish on large platter and spoon sauce over. Garnish with strips of chilli and coriander leaves. When buying the fish make sure it is no longer than your wok or frying pan.

KAO HORM MALI
STEAMED FRAGRANT RICE

See recipe in glossary.

FOI THONG
GOLDEN SILK

This elegant dish was introduced to the Thai court in the 16th century, during the golden era of the former capital Ayadhaya. It is essential to use duck eggs to strengthen the fine gold strips. Always make this dish a day in advance.

10 duck eggs
10 chicken eggs
1 kg (2 lbs) castor sugar
750 ml (3 cups) water
jasmine, violets or scented geranium leaves

Use three bowls for this procedure. Separate egg yolks into one bowl and egg whites into another. In the third bowl carefully scrape remaining egg white from shells. This egg white is rich in albumen and essential to the final appearance of 'golden silk'.

Strain egg yolks then the albumen from the third bowl through a fine sieve. Reserve the first bowl of egg whites. They can be frozen for later use.

Using a wide flat pan bring water to boil with sugar and simmer for 10 minutes until clear. Keep at simmering point. Prepare a small funnel from greaseproof paper and fill with egg yolk mixture or use a plastic ketchup dispenser, keeping your finger partially over the hole to adjust the stream.

Slowly dispense the egg yolk mixture into the simmering syrup, moving your hand in a circular motion. When the funnel is empty remove the egg threads with a slotted spoon. The egg mixture cooks rapidly. Repeat the process until all egg yolk mixture has been used. Add more boiling water to syrup if it thickens and the egg threads stick together.

Loosen strands with a fork and refrigerate overnight with jasmine, violets or scented geranium leaves. Remove flowers early next day before perfume deteriorates.

Serve on banana leaves cut to size or a silver platter. The stream of egg yolk mixture should be really fine.

LOY KRATONG DINNER

The festival of Kratong is celebrated at the full moon of the twelfth lunar month (November). In the early evening, young and old go to a waterway, any flowing water; a river, canal, lake or even a pond.

The tiny handmade floats are called kratong, made in the shape of a lotus flower containing a candle, incense stick, flowers and small coins. Candles are lit and the heavy perfume of incense fills the air as kratongs are placed in the water, with the prayers and secret wishes of their owners.

Thousands of flickering lights flow downstream carrying away each person's sins. If the candle remains alight prayers will be fulfilled.

The riverbanks and landings are crowded with people waiting to float their kratong in the water. Some are stopped by mischievous children scrambling through the water to steal coins from the floats. It is a magic night; the end of the monsoon season and the onset of cooler weather.

To dine in a place by the water under the stars with a full moon floating in the sky brings unforgettable memories.

On one such night, I cooked dinner to take to a friend's house on one of the main canals, where our floats made their journey slowly and safely.

I took duck salad with fresh sweet lychees (well worth peeling the fruit in season) combined with my hot soy sauce. The Chinese-inspired veal stew, delicately flavoured with star anise can be made in advance.

Green parcels of fish steamed while we had a pre-dinner drink and I stir-fried the spinach at the last minute.

Custard apple ice-cream was made the day before so I had plenty of time to pray and send my sins off on the kratong, while enjoying the energising powers of the full moon.

YAM PET OB
DUCK SALAD WITH LYCHEES

VEAL WITH STAR ANISE

PLA DOON BAI KLUAY
STEAMED FISH

PAK BUNG PAD KRATIEM
STIR-FRIED SPINACH WITH GARLIC

KAO HORM MALI
STEAMED FRAGRANT RICE

ICE-CREAM NOI NA
CUSTARD APPLE ICE-CREAM

YAM PET OB
DUCK SALAD WITH LYCHEES

1 no. 18 (3 lbs) whole roasted duck
4 red capsicum, or mixed, red, green and yellow
1 bunch watercress
40 ml (2 tablespoons) hot soy sauce
30 ml (1½ tablespoons) sesame oil
20 ml (1 tablespoon) wine vinegar
25 g (1 tablespoon) sugar
2 tins lychees
1 cup marinated ginger

Remove duck meat from bones and carcass, cut into strips and reserve. Cut capsicum into 2½ cm (1 inch) squares, blanch quickly in boiling water, refresh in cold water and drain. Wash watercress and cut off tough stems.

To make marinade:

Mix together hot soy sauce, sesame oil, wine vinegar, sugar, stir and add to blanched capsicum. Drain tinned lychees and reserve juice for later use (it is delicious).

Add ginger and lychees to marinade and toss in duck meat. Arrange watercress on a platter and top with duck salad.

Do not refrigerate duck as the skin is best when still crisp. Use fresh lychees in season after peeling skins.

VEAL WITH STAR ANISE

1 ½ kg (3 lbs) veal shoulder, boned
1 kg (2 lbs) pickling onions
½ celery stick
6 star anise
24 fresh or tinned green peppercorns
40 g (2 tablespoons) cornflour
salt to taste
40 ml (2 tablespoons) soy sauce
½ cup coriander leaves to garnish

Cube veal into 2½ cm (1 inch) pieces. Place in a saucepan, cover with cold water and slowly bring to boil. Remove from stove when scum rises to surface. Rinse veal under cold running water. Return blanched veal to saucepan with enough water to cover. Bring back to a slow simmer, covered with lid, for 30 minutes.

Peel small onions and leave whole. Cut celery into 5 cm (2 inch) lengths. Add onions, celery, star anise and peppercorns. Cover and simmer for 1 hour, or until veal is tender.

Dissolve cornflour in a little cold water and stir into veal to thicken the sauce. Season with salt and soy sauce. Garnish with coriander leaves and serve.

PLA DOON BAI KLUAY
STEAMED FISH

1 kg (2 lbs) white fish fillets
tumeric powder
1 teaspoon salt
dried chilli flakes
2 cloves garlic, finely chopped
1 teaspoon fresh green ginger, grated
2 shallots (red onions), chopped
1 tablespoon sesame oil
2 tablespoons coconut cream
4 shallots (red onions), cut into thin slices
16 soft lettuce leaves
banana leaves

Cut fish fillets into 8 pieces and rub with tumeric, salt and dried chilli flakes. Pound garlic, ginger, chopped shallots with sesame oil. Mix with coconut cream, and toss in thinly sliced shallots.

Spread 8 lettuce leaves on a flat surface, placing a small spoonful of paste on each one. Lay one piece of fish on each lettuce leaf. Spoon remaining paste on to fish pieces and cover with the other 8 lettuce leaves.

Wrap all 8 parcels in banana leaves and cook in bamboo steamer over boiling water for 30 minutes. Use cooking foil instead of banana leaves, if necessary. Serve still wrapped for each guest to enjoy full aroma.

PAK BUNG PAD KRATIEM
STIR-FRIED SPINACH WITH GARLIC

2 bunches of spinach
40 ml (2 tablespoons) bacon fat, duck fat or vegetable oil
6 cloves garlic, sliced thinly
fresh ground black pepper
20 ml (2 tablespoons) fish sauce

Living in the tropics, I buy Thai spinach, the runner variety which is easy to grow. In Thailand women wade knee-deep through water, picking the 30 cm (12 inch) long shoots. English spinach is the best substitute.

Remove tough stems from English spinach and wash in several lots of cold water to remove grit. Drain in colander. With Thai or runner spinach use stalks and leaves after washing carefully.

Heat fat or oil in wok and stir-fry garlic until coloured. Toss in spinach, turning over and over until it wilts. Add fresh ground pepper, fish sauce and toss quickly. Do not overcook spinach. Serve on platter.

KAO HORM MALI
STEAMED FRAGRANT RICE

See recipe in glossary.

ICE-CREAM NOI NA
CUSTARD APPLE ICE-CREAM

750 ml (3 cups) custard apple pulp
200 g (6½ oz) castor sugar
2 whole eggs
20 ml (2 tablespoons) lime juice
500 ml (2 cups) whipping cream

Slice open custard apples, scoop flesh into a sieve and push through removing pips. Extract 750 ml of pulp in a bowl, adding castor sugar. Beat the eggs with a fork, add to pulp with lime juice. Whip cream lightly and fold into mixture.

Churn in an ice-cream machine and place in freezer to set. Serve soft and creamy, not ice hard.

LUNCH AT PATHUM THANI

Wat Pai Lom, 'Temple of the Storks', is easily recognised from a boat on the river because of the large cranes circling in the air. The temple is surrounded by huge old trees with no foliage, where thousands of cranes nest each year. It is an eerie feeling to walk from the boat landing under the watchful eye of cranes in their nests. They fly off quietly, making no sound.

From the temple, it is a short trip down the Chao Phya river to Pathum Thani, 'lotus town'. The Mon people who came from Burma were given the town by the King as a place to live.

The area is famous for its rice noodles which are freshly made each day and shipped to Bangkok overnight. Even though noodle boats float along the river, after our temple visit we decided to lunch at a landing in town.

A platter of gleaming hot noodles was studded with bright green broccoli and served with a stack of crispy stir-fried bean sprouts.

Chicken thighs and fragrant black mushrooms combined in a casserole and came to the table with a basket of fish wings, steamed and served with a hot sauce of salted eggs.

Overlooking the busy market, we ate jackfruit with coconut custard, while longtailed boats unloaded farm produce. The minute they were empty, goods were taken aboard, to be carried up the river and into canals to where the farmers lived.

People lined up outside the restaurant waiting for a table, so we knew the food was fresh with such a big turnover.

A good point to remember when visiting Thailand, is to look for a restaurant filled with locals, you can be sure it is the best place in town.

GWAYTIO RAD NAR
NOODLES WITH BROCCOLI AND PRAWNS

PAD TUA NGORK
STIR-FRIED BEAN SPROUTS

TOM KEM GAI
CASSEROLE OF CHICKEN THIGHS AND MUSHROOMS

PLA DOON
STEAMED FISH WINGS

NAM PRIK KAI KEM
SALTED EGG SAUCE

KAO HORM MALI
STEAMED FRAGRANT RICE

SANKAYA GAB KANOON
COCONUT CUSTARD WITH JACKFRUIT

GWAYTIO RAD NAR
NOODLES WITH BROCCOLI AND PRAWNS

½ kg (1 lb) fresh rice noodles (sold in Asian food shops)
250 g (8 oz) broccoli (western or Chinese)
40 ml (2 tablespoons) vegetable oil
4 cloves garlic, chopped
250 g (8 oz) cooked prawns, shelled and deveined
250 ml (1 cup) fish or chicken stock
60 ml (3 tablespoons) oyster sauce
30 ml (1 ½ tablespoons) fish sauce
20 g (1 tablespoon) sugar
10 g (2 teaspoons) cornflour, dissolved in a little water
½ teaspoon dried chilli flakes to garnish

Fresh noodles come in a big sheet, folded over. Cut the bundle into 10 mm (½ inch) strips and separate. Slice broccoli diagonally into 5 cm (2 inch) pieces. Blanch in boiling water and refresh in cold, to retain green colour.

Heat oil in wok and fry garlic for 1 minute. Add noodles and toss. Add broccoli, prawns and stock and bring to boil. Stir in oyster sauce, fish sauce and sugar. Thicken stock with cornflour and stir well, cooking through. Turn on to a platter and sprinkle with chilli flakes.

PAD TUA NGORK
STIR-FRIED BEAN SPROUTS

40 ml (2 tablespoons) vegetable oil
5 cloves garlic, thinly sliced
250 g (8 oz) cooked prawns, shelled and deveined
30 ml (1 ½ tablespoons) fish sauce
½ teaspoon dried chilli flakes
250 g fresh bean sprouts, cleaned

Heat oil in wok and fry garlic until crisp and golden. Add prawns, fish sauce, dried chilli flakes and bean sprouts. Toss to stir-fry for 2 minutes. Serve immediately before bean sprouts go soft.

Clockwise from top: Som Or Polemo: Carved water melon; Malakor: Carved papaya; Lamoot Sapodilla; Foie Thong: Golden silk; Kanoon: Jack fruit.

TOM KEM GAI
CASSEROLE OF CHICKEN THIGHS AND MUSHROOMS

8 chicken thighs, skin removed
8 Chinese mushrooms
8 small pickling onions, peeled
8 hard-boiled eggs, peeled
1 medium onion, chopped
3 cloves garlic, crushed
1 cm (½ inch) fresh ginger, peeled and chopped
2 coriander roots, chopped
½ teaspoon salt
12 peppercorns
40 ml (2 tablespoons) vegetable oil
50 g (2 tablespoons) brown sugar or palm sugar
30 ml (1 ½ tablespoons) light soy sauce
250 ml (1 cup) water
coriander leaves to garnish

Soak mushrooms in hot water for 1 hour. Discard woody stems. Pound medium onion, garlic, ginger, coriander roots, salt and peppercorns to a coarse paste. Heat oil in wok and fry paste for 5 minutes.

Discard paste, leaving spicy flavoured oil in base of wok. Add sugar and stir to caramelise. Add soy sauce and water, bringing to boil. Add chicken thighs, mushrooms, small onions and simmer, covered, for 45 minutes. Add hard-boiled eggs and cook for another 30 minutes. Garnish with coriander leaves and serve.

Kanom Kluk: Coconut pancakes.

PLA DOON
STEAMED FISH WINGS

In this simple dish, flavoured by the salted egg sauce, use any white fish fillets. I like to use fish wings which are the most delicious part of the fish.

Allow one fish wing for each guest. Clean and scale. Place in a shallow dish or on a piece of cooking foil, in a bamboo steamer and cook over boiling water for 15 minutes or until fish comes away from bone. Remove to a serving platter. Each guest flavours the fish with Nam Prik Kai Kem to taste (see next recipe).

NAM PRIK KAI KEM
SALTED EGG SAUCE

3 shallots (red onions), chopped
4 fresh red chillis, chopped
4 cloves garlic, chopped
6 hard-boiled eggs, preferably salted eggs (see glossary)
2 teaspoons shrimp paste
1 tablespoon brown sugar or palm sugar
40 ml (2 tablespoons) fish sauce
40 ml (2 tablespoons) lime juice

Pound shallots, chillis and garlic into a paste. Add hard-boiled eggs pounding well with shrimp paste and sugar, using a rotating movement. Stir in fish sauce and lime juice. Serve as a dipping sauce for steamed fish.

This sauce is rich in protein and is often used to flavour a bowl of plain boiled rice.

KAO HORM MALI
STEAMED FRAGRANT RICE

See recipe in glossary.

SANKAYA GAB KANOON
COCONUT CUSTARD WITH JACKFRUIT

400 ml (1 ½ cups) coconut milk
3 large eggs
3 egg yolks
50 g (2 tablespoons) brown sugar
20 g (2 teaspoons) cornflour
200 g jackfruit flesh, chopped coarsely

Heat coconut milk in a double boiler. Whisk whole eggs, egg yolks, sugar and cornflour until thick and creamy. Add to warm coconut milk stirring well. Add jackfruit stirring constantly. When thickened pour into individual dishes or young coconut shells.

Place containers in a bamboo steamer, over boiling water. Steam for 40 minutes or until custard is set. Serve to your taste, hot, tepid or chilled.

Jackfruit has a more crunchy texture when fresh. Use the canned variety as a substitute.

LUNCH IN AYUTTHAYA

The former capital of the Kingdom of Siam, Ayutthaya, founded in 1350, was the centre of trade between India and china.

Silk, copper and tea were exchanged for pepper and rare timber. Built on an island surrounded on four sides by rivers, it was a walled city with magnificent temples and elaborate palaces. Gilded spires and pagodas shone in the sunlight. European travellers wrote of its splendour, describing it as a water-borne city floating on a giant river, richly ornamented by its kings and people.

In 1767 the Burmese sacked the city, and an entire civilisation went up in flames. Most of the buildings were burned to the ground, but the ruins bear witness to a rich bygone era.

To visit Ayutthaya, it is best to hire a car and driver and leave Bangkok early in the morning. See the ruins while the morning is still cool. Then drive to King Chulalongkorn's summer palace, Bang Pa-In, on the river, surrounded by beautiful gardens with elegant topiary in the shape of animals. Board the *Oriental Queen* at the boat landing for an exciting cruise down the river, bustling with activities. The boat arrives back at the Oriental Hotel by sunset.

On my early visits, I enjoyed lunch at a restaurant with a 'nipa' thatched roof, built on stilts in the river.

As an appetiser we were served a salad of stir-fried cabbage which had a crunchy, refreshing taste.

There was a tureen of steaming corn and crabmeat soup, delicate in flavour, in contrast to the chilli chicken. Tender snake beans, which are easy to grow, quickly stir-fried with pork completed the repast.

We drank icy cold Singha beer from glass mugs, and after lunch were driven back to Bangkok, dozing most of the way.

YAM GALUMBLEE
STIR-FRIED CABBAGE SALAD

GAENG CHUD KAOPOT AUN
CORN AND CRABMEAT SOUP

MOO PAD TUA FAK YAW
STIR-FRIED PORK WITH SNAKE BEANS

GAI-OB PRIK-PAOW
CHICKEN WITH CHILLI PASTE

KAO HORM MALI
STEAMED FRAGRANT RICE

MAMUANG TORD
FRIED MANGO

YAM GALUMBLEE
STIR-FRIED CABBAGE SALAD

1 small head of white cabbage, or ½ large cabbage
40 ml (2 tablespoons) vegetable oil
8 cloves garlic, thinly sliced
8 shallots (red onions), thinly sliced
4 fresh red chillis, cut into strips
40 ml (2 tablespoons) fish sauce
40 ml fresh lime juice
125 ml (½ cup) coconut milk
roasted peanuts, crushed, to garnish

Heat oil in a skillet and fry garlic until crisp. Remove with a slotted spoon and set aside. Repeat with shallots and chilli strips. Cut cabbage into quarters and slice thinly. Blanch cabbage quickly in a large pot of boiling water and drain in a colander. Mix lime juice, fish sauce and coconut milk in a bowl, add cabbage and toss well.

Turn on to a serving platter and garnish with crisp fried garlic, onions and chillis. Crush roasted peanuts and sprinkle over cabbage for added flavour.

GAENG CHUD KAOPOT AUN
CORN AND CRABMEAT SOUP

2 litres (8 cups) chicken stock or clear fish stock
5 cloves garlic, chopped
5 shallots (red onions), chopped
30 ml (1½ tablespoons) vegetable oil
40 ml (2 tablespoons) fish sauce
250 g (8 oz) cooked crabmeat
250 g (8 oz) fresh young corn kernels
2 whole eggs beaten with a little cold stock
1 tablespoon cracked·black peppercorns to garnish
2 tablespoons coriander leaves to garnish

Heat stock in a large saucepan. Fry garlic and shallots in hot oil until golden brown. Add to stock with fish sauce, crabmeat and corn kernels. Bring to boil. Whisk in eggs beaten with stock and simmer for 1 minute.

Pour into soup tureen, and serve garnished with crushed black peppercorns and coriander leaves.

MOO PAD TUA FAK YAW
STIR-FRIED PORK WITH SNAKE BEANS

400 g (13 oz) pork loin, thinly sliced and cut into small pieces
8 cloves garlic, sliced thinly
40 ml (2 tablespoons) vegetable oil
500 g (1 lb) snake beans or string beans, cut into 5 mm (¼ inch) lengths
50 ml (2½ tablespoons) fish sauce
10 g (2 teaspoons) brown sugar
freshly ground pepper

Heat oil in a wok and stir-fry garlic until it starts to colour. Add thinly sliced pork and stir-fry with garlic for 1 minute. Add beans and toss for no longer than 2 minutes. Add fish sauce, sugar and freshly ground pepper, tossing quickly.

Turn on to a platter and serve immediately. The beans should be green and crisp.

GAI OB PRIK-PAOW
CHICKEN WITH CHILLI PASTE

1 no. 16 or 18 (4 lbs) fresh chicken
10 cloves garlic, sliced thinly
60 g (3 tablespoons) chilli paste
40 ml (2 tablespoons) honey
40 ml (2 tablespoons) soy sauce
40 ml (2 tablespoons) vegetable oil

Cut chicken into quarters and then into 8 pieces. Mix together garlic, chilli paste, honey and soy sauce, rub well into chicken. Leave to marinate for 2 hours.

Pre-heat oven to 220°C (440°F). Spread chicken evenly in roasting pan and sprinkle with oil. Place in hot oven, turning from time to time. Cook for 30 minutes. The chicken skin should be crisp. If not, crisp chicken under broiler, watching carefully to see it does not burn. Serve on platter as part of a meal.

KAO HORM MALI
STEAMED FRAGRANT RICE

See recipe in glossary.

MAMUANG TORD
FRIED MANGO

4 fresh ripe mangoes
50g (2 tablespoons) unsalted butter
100 g (5 tablespoons) brown sugar or palm sugar
4 limes, cut into slices

Remove skins from mangoes with a vegetable peeler. Slice fruit from the stone. Heat butter in frying pan until it turns nut brown. Fry mango slices for 2 minutes on each side. Place mangoes on individual dishes.

Add sugar to remaining butter in frying pan. Stir until dissolved and like a syrup. Divide sauce evenly over mangoes. Serve with slices of lime for guests to squeeze over fruit to their taste.

ROSEGARDEN LUNCH

On the way to Nakorn Pathom, with its magnificent golden pagoda, an hour's drive from Bangkok, is the 'Rosegarden'. Many hectares of parkland, by the river and lakes, have gardens filled with thousands of rose bushes. They bloom profusely in the warm sunshine, perfuming the air away from the city's pollution.

Traditional Thai timber houses are set amongst the gardens and along the riverside, where guests can stay for a holiday. In the park there is a Thai artisans' village where you can watch the craftsmen at work; weavers, silversmiths and wood carvers.

There are floating kitchens along the river and from the noodle boat you can have the most delicious bowl of Ba Mee Nam. Thin egg noodles float in a rich stock, topped with sliced chicken, pork or fish balls (Look Cheen), sprinkled with a mixture of sugar, crushed peanuts and chilli flakes. Quite a meal by itself.

My favourite place to have lunch is the floating restaurant anchored at the riverside.

On my last visit with friends, we chose a refreshing salad of flaked pomelo topped with lots of deep red fragrant rose petals; it was always hard to pass the fried stuffed crab.

We feasted on a platter of spicy chicken wings and succulent fresh river prawns, steamed and served in a bamboo basket. We used our fingers and rinsed them in finger bowls which had floating jasmine flowers.

To finish we chose fresh lychees in creamy custard. At the end of lunch we refreshed our faces and hands with hot towels.

The rest of the afternoon was spent watching the shows in the main part of the gardens; traditional classical dancing and Thai boxing.

BA MEE NAM
EGG NOODLE SOUP

YAM SOM-OR
POMELO SALAD WITH SHRIMPS

POO CHA
FRIED STUFFED CRAB

PEEK GAI OB
SPICY CHICKEN WINGS

GOONG DOON
STEAMED RIVER PRAWNS

KAO HORM MALI
STEAMED FRAGRANT RICE

LEENCHEE LOI MEK
LYCHEES IN CUSTARD SAUCE

BA MEE NAM
EGG NOODLE SOUP

250 g (8 oz) Ba Mee noodles (thin egg noodles sold in Asian food shops)
150 g (5 oz) fresh bean sprouts
8 cloves garlic, thinly sliced and fried crisp
2 litres (8 cups) chicken stock
8 thin slices of red pork, cut into strips
8 cooked prawns, peeled and deveined
4 lettuce leaves, shredded
40 ml (2 tablespoons) fish sauce
3 spring onions, sliced thinly
20 g (1 tablespoon) sugar
40 g (2 tablespoons) roasted peanuts, crushed
dried chilli flakes to garnish
coriander leaves to garnish

Cook noodles in salted boiling water for 12 minutes. Drain in a colander and turn into tureen. Add bean sprouts and crisp-fried garlic. Heat chicken stock and add pork, prawns, lettuce and fish sauce. Heat through and pour over noodles. Garnish with spring onions, sugar, crushed peanuts, chilli flakes and coriander leaves.

YAM SOM-OR
POMELO SALAD WITH SHRIMPS

1 pomelo
400 g (13 oz) small prawns or shrimps, cooked, peeled and deveined
3 cloves garlic, finely crushed
20 ml (1 tablespoon) fresh lime juice
20 ml (1 tablespoon) fish sauce
½ teaspoon dried chilli flakes, or more to taste
20 mint leaves to garnish

Remove thick skin from pomelo and divide into sections. Peel white membrane from each section with a small knife. Flake fruit carefully into a bowl. Mix garlic, lime juice and fish sauce together, pour over pomelo. Toss in prawns and garnish with chilli flakes and mint leaves before serving.

POO CHA
FRIED STUFFED CRAB

8 top shells from sea crabs
220 g (7 oz) crab meat, cooked
220 g (7 oz) pork fillet or lean pork
3 shallots, (red onions) peeled
3 cloves garlic, peeled
2.5 cm (1 inch) fresh ginger, peeled
2 coriander roots
185 ml (¾ cup) coconut cream
25 g (1 tablespoon) cornflour
2 eggs, lightly beaten
salt to taste
fresh ground pepper
oil for frying
sweet chilli sauce to serve

Add pork, shallots, garlic, ginger and coriander roots to food processor bowl. Chop until combined, or pass ingredients twice through a meat grinder. Place in a bowl with crab meat. Stir in coconut cream and cornflour mixed with the eggs. Season with salt and pepper and mix well together.

Divide mixture into 8 crab shells and place in bamboo steamer. Place over boiling water to steam for ½ hour.

When ready to serve, shallow fry in hot oil, shell-side up, until golden brown. Serve at once with sweet chilli sauce, found in bottles at Asian food stores.

PEEK GAI OB
SPICY CHICKEN WINGS

1 kg chicken wings, using upper bone joining breast
2–3 fresh red chillis, chopped finely
100 ml (5 tablespoons) tomato paste
40 ml (2 tablespoons) soy sauce
100 ml (5 tablespoons) vegetable oil
40 ml (2 tablespoons) vinegar
2½ cm (1 inch) fresh green ginger, peeled and finely chopped or
    1 tablespoon marinated ginger, finely chopped
3 cloves garlic, finely chopped
coriander leaves to garnish

Remove wing tips and reserve. Using upper chicken wing, scrape flesh back towards the thick end with a small knife. This leaves the bone exposed to use as a handle.

To make marinade:

Mix all remaining ingredients together in a stainless steel or glass bowl. Add chicken to marinade, turning until well coated. Allow to stand overnight in the refrigerator.

   Heat oven to 220°C (400°F). Spread chicken wings evenly in a roasting pan, baste with marinade. Cook for 20 minutes, turning and basting once or twice. Serve on a platter, garnished with coriander leaves, as part of a meal.

GOONG DOON
STEAMED RIVER PRAWNS

Choose two prawns depending on size, for each guest. Place in a bamboo basket and steam over boiling water until pink and cooked, about 10 to 15 minutes.

Sauce

4 fresh red chillis, chopped
2.5 cm (1 inch) fresh green ginger, peeled and chopped
125 g (4 oz) sugar
125 ml (½ cup) water
20 ml (1 tablespoon) fish sauce

Bring all ingredients to boil and simmer for 5 minutes. Allow to cool and serve with prawns as a dipping sauce.

KAO HORM MALI
STEAMED FRAGRANT RICE

See recipe in glossary.

LEENCHEE LOI MEK
LYCHEES IN CUSTARD SAUCE

24 fresh lychees, or tinned
4 egg yolks
50 g (2 oz) sugar
250 ml (1 cup) light cream

Whisk egg yolks, sugar and cream together and place in a double boiler. Stir until mixture coats the back of a spoon. Allow to cool. Peel lychees and remove stone. Place lychees in the custard and chill. Serve 3 lychees in custard to each guest.

LAMPHUN LUNCH

The road to Lamphun from Chiangmai, in the north of Thailand, is lined with 15 kilometres of trees. Old and majestic, they grow on each side of the road, their branches meeting in a bower overhead, providing coolness and shade for the traveller. The road passes through orchards of longan, much prized in Bangkok markets, lush green fields of garlic, groundnuts and tobacco.

Haripunchai, for 621 years was a Mon kingdom until it was captured by King Mangrai of Chiangmai in 1281. The town is rich in monuments and magnificent temples, with some of the best examples of religious architecture in Thailand, particularly Wat Haripunchai. The city is famous for its hand-woven silks, with brilliant colours, intricate designs and exquisite embroidery.

The nearby village of Pa Sang, whose inhabitants are of Mons descent, is known for its cotton weaving and the sound of 'click-clack' from thousands of looms fills the air. The girls who live here are so beautiful it is said many men come to buy cotton and leave with a wife.

In Lamphun I had lunch at the house of a friend whose family dates back to a famous Thai queen, Chami Devi. The wooden house was entirely covered with intricate carvings, only the floorboards were not decorated.

We were served a salad of pork skin flavoured with herbs and a bowl of sticky rice; we made little balls of rice with our fingers and dipped them into the salad.

Green spears of fresh asparagus were tossed in soy sauce and the finely chopped chicken had a spicy, chilli-hot taste; it was to be mixed with sticky rice and dipped in sauce.

The wild boar curry was an interesting addition to the menu. This style of curry is often made only with vegetables. In remote and mountainous parts of Thailand there are no coconut palms and, therefore, coconut milk is not used.

There was a silver tureen filled with chicken wing soup blended with Chinese dates, to cool the palate. To finish, a watermelon, hollowed out and carved, was filled with the most delicious fruit of the season.

YAM NANG MOO
PORK SKIN SALAD

STIR-FRIED ASPARAGUS

GAI PAD BAI GRA-PAO
STIR-FRIED RED CHICKEN

GAENG CHUD GAI
CHICKEN WING SOUP

GAENG BA
WILD BOAR CURRY

KAO HORM MALI
STEAMED FRAGRANT RICE

EXOTIC FRUIT SALAD

YAM NANG MOO
PORK SKIN SALAD

Quantity of pork skin 600 g (20 oz)

SAUCE

2 stalks of lemon grass, tender part only, finely chopped
5 makrut leaves, chopped
6 shallots (red onions), finely chopped
½ cup mint leaves
½ cup coriander leaves
1 teaspoon dried chilli flakes
40 ml (2 tablespoons) fish sauce
2 teaspoons sugar

Use pork skin reserved from Sweet Pork and other recipes, approximately 600 g (20 oz). Place pork skin in a saucepan of water. Bring to boil and simmer until skin is tender. Allow to cool in water. Remove, drain and slice into thin strips. Cut across strips to dice the skin. Place in a bowl.

To make salad:

Add all ingredients to bowl of pork skin, mixing well together. Refrigerate for 1 hour to allow pork skin to absorb flavours. Turn on to serving platter. This is a delicious salad with a most unusual texture.

STIR-FRIED ASPARAGUS

500 g (1 lb) fresh green thin asparagus spears
30 ml (1 ½ tablespoons) vegetable oil
5 cloves garlic, thinly sliced
60 ml (3 tablespoons) oyster sauce
1 teaspoon crushed green peppercorns, fresh or tinned
20 ml (1 tablespoon) fish sauce
20 g (1 tablespoon) sugar

Slice asparagus spears into 3 pieces. Heat oil in wok and fry garlic slices until golden. Add asparagus and stir-fry. Add oyster sauce, peppercorns, fish sauce, sugar and stir-fry for 2 minutes. Turn on to platter and serve.

GAI PAD BAI GRA-PAO
STIR-FRIED RED CHICKEN

500 g (1 lb) meat from chicken legs, cut into small pieces or chopped
   coarsely with a cleaver
40 ml (2 tablespoons) mirin or dry sherry
10 fresh red chillis, roasted until black
40 g (2 tablespoons) shrimp paste
2 teaspoons salt
oil for frying
6 shallots (red onions), thinly sliced
8 cloves garlic, thinly sliced
3 large tomatoes, peeled, seeded and diced
½ cup sweet basil leaves

Mix chopped chicken meat with mirin or dry sherry and allow to marinate
for 2 hours. Pound the roasted chillis with shrimp paste and salt to a
smooth paste. Fry shallots in oil until brown and crisp. Repeat process with
garlic. Drain and reserve.

Using the same oil, fry chilli paste until fragrant. Add chicken with mirin
and stir-fry for 3 minutes. Add diced tomatoes and mix together. Toss in
onions, garlic and basil, stir to mix through. Turn on to a platter and serve.

GAENG BA
WILD BOAR CURRY

1 kg (2 lb) leg of wild boar or loin of boar; pork or beef
   rump can also be used
125 ml (½ cup) vegetable oil
3 tablespoons gaeng ba paste
6–8 fresh chillis, any colour
40 ml (2 tablespoons) fish sauce
2 makrut leaves or kaffir lime leaves, torn
1 tablespoon raw sugar
20 basil leaves

Slice meat very, very thin. Heat oil in wok and fry gaeng ba paste for a few seconds. Add 1 litre (4 cups) water and bring to boil. Add meat slices, chillis and cook for 10 minutes. Season with fish sauce, makrut leaves, sugar and basil leaves.

This curry is often served with sliced bamboo shoots, or eggplant and capsicum. Add your own choice of vegetables.

GAENG BA CURRY PASTE

10 red chillis
3 shallots (red onions), chopped
1 piece galangal 2½ cm (1 inch), peeled and chopped
1 piece fresh ginger 2½ cm (1 inch), peeled and chopped
2 makrut leaves, chopped
3 stalks lemon grass, tender part only, chopped
zest of 2 limes

Mix all ingredients together in food processor or pound to a paste in mortar. Store in a glass jar in refrigerator.

GAENG CHUD GAI
CHICKEN WING SOUP

8 chicken wings
2 litres (8 cups) chicken stock
8 dried Chinese mushrooms
16 dried Chinese dates
1 celery stalk, sliced finely

Pour boiling water over mushrooms and soak for 40 minutes. Discard hard stems. Place chicken wings in a clay pot with mushrooms, dates and celery. Bring chicken stock to boil and pour over chicken wings.

Cover with lid and place in pre-heated oven, 200°C (400°F), for 40 minutes. Remove from oven to table and open before guests. The aroma from the pot is heavenly.

KAO HORM MALI
STEAMED FRAGRANT RICE

See recipe in glossary.

EXOTIC FRUIT SALAD

250 ml (1 cup) water
250 g (½ lb) sugar
lime or lemon zest

Add sugar to water in a saucepan, with zest of lime or lemon, bring to boil and cook for five minutes. Lime or lemon zest adds a refreshing flavour. To prepare watermelon, slice rind along the top to make a lid. Use a melon baller to remove fruit and place in a large bowl. Scoop out remaining watermelon to make a bowl in which to serve the fruit salad.

With a melon baller scoop fruit from honey dew and cantaloupe. Dice babacos, papaya, mango and pepinos. Peel and stone lychees, add to bowl with Brazilian cherries.

Pour cold simple syrup over fruit salad mix and chill for 1 hour. To serve, spoon fruit into watermelon bowl, and garnish with mint leaves.

This fruit salad will be fragrant enough without the addition of liqueur. A fresh finale to a summer meal.

ROYAL ORCHID DINNER

I found the most beautiful description of Thailand on an old stone tablet in the ancient capital of Sukhotai, dated the year 1292, the time of King Ramkhamhaeng. It read:

'This Sukhotai is good
In the water there is fish
In the field there is rice
The King takes no advantage of the people
Who wants to trade, trades
The faces of the people shine bright with happiness'.

In reading this you will understand my love of Thailand and its people. The people of Thailand make the country as great as it is. A people deeply involved in tradition. The traditions of the past are essential to them; without these traditions there would be no present and no future.

Thai International Airlines has kept these traditions in twenty-five years of flying. The crew provide traditional service and their faces 'shine bright with happiness'. I am pleased to have contributed dishes served on board flights leaving Australia and include some of my own recipes for this last menu.

To conclude I would like to quote a Lahu legend which the hilltribe people tell to their children:

'The earth was created a little too large
And the heaven a little too small
Strings were attached to the four corners of the earth
And were drawn, forming hills and valleys
Rocks and stones were put in
Seeds of trees and plants were sown
To make birds happy and sing of joy
The hills in their beauty shone'.

I wish you lots of happy cooking and 'Sawadee Krup'.

SALAD OF DRIED SHRIMPS AND CELERY

FISH BAKED WITH BLACK BEAN SAUCE

STEAMED VELVET LEMON CHICKEN

KAO HORM MALI
STEAMED FRAGRANT RICE

MANGO PARFAIT

SALAD OF DRIED SHRIMPS AND CELERY

125 g (4 oz) dried shrimps
80 ml (4 tablespoons) dry sherry or sake
80 ml (4 tablespoons) boiling water
heart of celery, using inner white stalks
2 teaspoons salt
2 teaspoons Szechuan pepper oil (found in Asian food
    stores)

Place dried shrimps in a bowl and pour over sherry or sake. Leave to soak overnight or at least 8 hours. Half an hour before serving, add boiling water, toss well and allow to stand.

Remove threads from celery stalks and cut on a slant about 1 cm (½ inch) thick. This should make about 4 cups of celery. Toss celery with salt in a bowl. Place in a bamboo steamer over boiling water; steam for 6 minutes. Rinse under cold water and drain.

Pour shrimps and liquid over celery. Add Szechuan pepper oil and toss well. Cover and chill.

When ready to serve, spoon salad into individual serving dishes or lacquer bowls with lids. Place bowls at each table setting to be eaten during the meal.

FISH BAKED WITH BLACK BEAN SAUCE

This is one of my favourite fish dishes, and evolved through my love of Asian cooking. It is often served on Thai International Airlines. The sauce can be prepared in advance and kept refrigerated in a jar. Only a small amount is required for each serving of fish.

8 pieces of firm white fish fillets, jewfish, ling
   or coral trout

Sauce ingredients

125 ml (½ cup) vegetable oil
3 cloves garlic, finely chopped
125 ml (½ cup) fermented black beans, well rinsed
2 shallots (red onions), thinly sliced
½ teaspoon red chilli flakes
125 ml (½ cup) water
1 tablespoon soy sauce
1 tablespoon mirin or dry sherry
½ teaspoon sugar
½ teaspoon sesame oil
2 teaspoons cornflour

To prepare sauce:

Heat oil in wok and fry garlic, black beans, shallots, and chilli flakes for 30 seconds. Mix together water, soy sauce, mirin or sherry, sugar, sesame oil and blend with cornflour. Add mixture to wok, stir and simmer for 1 minute. Remove and store in jar until needed.

To cook fish:

Butter 8 pieces of cooking foil and sprinkle with salt and pepper. Place 1 fillet of fish on each piece of foil and top with 1 teaspoon of black bean sauce. Close foil tightly and bake in hot oven (220°C or 450°F) for approximately 10 to 12 minutes. Remove from foil and serve.

STEAMED VELVET LEMON CHICKEN

Another of my favourite dishes, also served on Thai International flights. This is a good dish for parties as it requires minimum work after guests have arrived. I use the Chinese preparation of velveting the chicken, a useful technique to learn and ideal for steaming. The chicken can be deep fried in oil, but only for 40 seconds, and should stay white.

1 kg (2 lbs) chicken meat, breast or thighs, cut into bite-size pieces

Velveting Marinade:

2 egg whites
2 tablespoons cornflour
2 tablespoons mirin or dry sherry
1 teaspoon salt
2 tablespoons peanut oil

Sauce:

4 tablespoons hoisin sauce
4 tablespoons black bean paste
2 tablespoons light soy sauce
2 tablespoons dry sherry
2 teaspoons sugar
½ teaspoon salt
2 tablespoons lemon juice
2 teaspoons grated lemon peel
2 tablespoons vegetable oil
16 slices lemon, paper thin
coriander leaves for garnish

To prepare Marinade:

Beat egg whites until broken but not frothy. Stir in cornflour, mirin or sherry, adding salt and peanut oil. Use as a marinade for fish, prawns, chicken, turkey, veal or pork.

To prepare Lemon Chicken:

Toss chicken pieces in Velveting Marinade.

To make Sauce:

Mix together sauce ingredients until smooth. Place velvet chicken pieces on a platter, evenly spread out. Spoon sauce over chicken and surround with lemon slices. Place in a bamboo steamer over boiling water. Steam for 20 to 30 minutes. Garnish with coriander leaves.

KAO HORM MALI
STEAMED FRAGRANT RICE

See recipe in glossary.

MANGO PARFAIT

4–5 mangoes, peeled and puréed to make ½ litre (2 cups)
150 g (5 oz) castor sugar
5 egg yolks
juice of 1 lemon
10 ml (2 teaspoons) kirsch
325 ml (1 ½ cups) whipping cream
sprig of pineapple sage or
   mint to garnish

Mango Sauce:

2 ripe mangoes, peeled and puréed
60 g (2 oz) castor sugar
10 ml (2 teaspoons kirsch)

Pass the mango purée through a sieve. Place in a saucepan with sugar and cook over a low heat for 10 to 15 minutes until mixture becomes transparent.

Beat egg yolks in a copper bowl over a double boiler. Add mango mixture and continue to whisk until thickened. Place copper bowl immediately over crushed ice to stop any further cooking. Add lemon juice, kirsch and leave to chill. Whip cream lightly and fold into mango mixture.

Pour into ice-cream maker and churn. Line a terrine mould or bread tin with 3 or 4 layers of greaseproof paper. Place mould in freezer to chill. Remove ice-cream from churn and turn into paper-lined mould and freeze overnight.

To make Sauce:

Place all ingredients in food processor and blend together. Chill.

To serve, turn parfait from mould and cut into 2.5 cm (1 inch) slices. Pour 2 tablespoons of mango sauce on each plate. Place parfait slice on the sauce. Garnish with a sprig of pineapple sage or mint.

INDEX